RUABON TO BARMOUTH

Vic Mitchell and Keith Smith

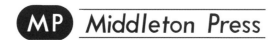

MP Middleton Press

Front cover: Approaching Dolgelley on 12th August 1935 is 2-6-0 no. 6399 with a Barmouth to Ruabon train. The River Mawddach is close by. (H.F.Wheeller/R.S.Carpenter coll.)

Back cover upper: Waiting at Llanuwchllyn is class 4 4-6-0 no. 75029, not long before line closure. The Bala Lake Railway now operates from here. (Colour-Rail.com)

Back cover lower: The Llangollen Railway re-enacted the Rainhill Trials when Sans Pareil *and* Novelty *were steamed at Carrog on 3rd October 2002. (T.Heavyside)*

Published September 2010

ISBN 978 1 906008 84 0

© Middleton Press, 2010

Design Deborah Esher

Published by
>   *Middleton Press*
>   *Easebourne Lane*
>   *Midhurst*
>   *West Sussex*
>   *GU29 9AZ*
Tel: 01730 813169
Fax: 01730 812601
Email: info@middletonpress.co.uk
www.middletonpress.co.uk

Printed in the United Kingdom by Henry Ling Limited, at the Dorset Press, Dorchester, DT1 1HD

INDEX

ACKNOWLEDGEMENTS

We are very grateful for the assistance received from many of those mentioned in the credits also to L.Crosier, G.Croughton, T.Hancock, R.Hawkes, J.B.Horne, S.C.Jenkins, M.A.N.Johnston, N.Langridge, J.H.Meredith, A.Rhodes, K.Robinson, Mr D and Dr S.Salter, L.Turner, M.Turvey, T.Walsh and particularly our ever supportive wives, Barbara Mitchell and Janet Smith.

I. GWR route in 1932. (Railway Magazine).

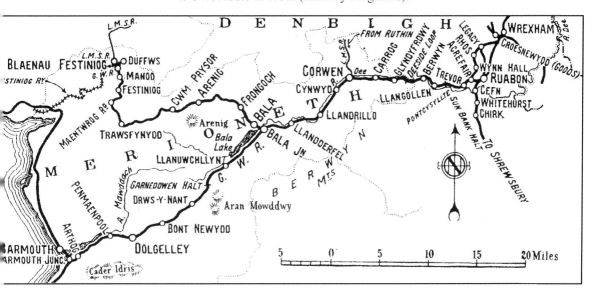

GEOGRAPHICAL SETTING

After the first stop, Acrefair, we drop down into the Vale of Llangollen and run close to the east flowing River Dee for around 30 miles. It enters the sea five miles north of Chester. The line has an undulating profile and rises only about 100ft in its first 25 miles.

The watershed is reached after 35 miles and a steep descent in the valley of the Afon Wnion begins. (Avon Onion is often said). This fast flowing river reaches the wider Afon Mawddach near Penmaenpool. This becomes even wider as it approaches the sea, the route being on its south side. Trains still cross its estuary on its famous wooden bridge to reach Barmouth.

The line was built on the Denbighshire/Shropshire border for its first ten miles, the remainder being in Merionethshire, the county town of which was Dolgelley. West and north of here are some gold deposits, which have been worked periodically. Ancient sedimentary rocks form the underlying geology for most of the route, but there is much volcanic rock in the area. One of the most significant geological fault lines in Britain runs close to the route and is known as the Bala Fault.

The maps are to the scale of 25ins to 1 mile, with north at the top unless otherwise indicated. Welsh spelling and hyphenation has varied over the years and so we have generally used the form used by the railways at the time.

Gradient Profile

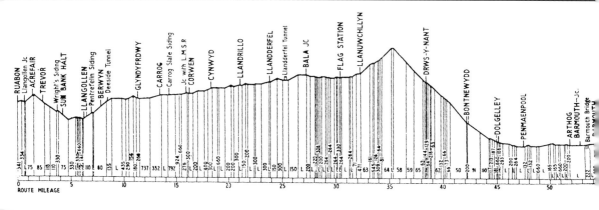

HISTORICAL BACKGROUND

The northern part of the Shrewsbury & Chester Railway was opened through Ruabon in 1846 and a branch from it to Llangollen was brought into use by the Vale of Llangollen Railway on 2nd June 1862. Its Act was dated 1st August 1859. The former became part of the Great Western Railway in 1854.

The Llangollen & Corwen Railway opened on 8th May 1865, a line having arrived at Corwen from the north, via Ruthin, in 1864. The Corwen & Bala Railway followed on westwards on 6th July 1866. The Bala & Dolgelley Railway began operating on 4th August 1868, and became a constituent of the GWR in 1877 and the other three followed in 1896. The branch from the route to Bala itself came in 1882, when the line to Festiniog opened. The GWR worked all these lines from their opening.

The Aberystwyth & Welsh Coast Railway started services between Llwyngwril and Penmaenpool on 3rd July 1865. It became part of the Cambrian Railways that year. This company opened the route from Barmouth Junction to Pwllheli on 3rd June 1867 and the link from Penmaenpool to Dolgelley on 21st June 1869. There were two separate stations here until January 1872. The CR was absorbed by the GWR in 1922, it having doubled the section east of Llangollen in 1898-1900.

With the advent of nationalisation, all lines in the area became part of the Western Region of British Railways on 1st January 1948. The route was transferred to the London Midland Region on 17th June 1963.

The line north of Corwen lost its passenger service in 1953, but Land Cruise trains used it until freight ceased in April 1962.

The Ruabon-Barmouth service was scheduled for withdrawal on 18th January 1965, but nature intervened and flood damage on 12th December 1964 resulted in cessation of traffic between Llangollen and Barmouth. On 14th December 1964, service was restored between Bala and Barmouth, with a reversal at Bala Junction. (The route to Blaenau Ffestiniog had closed in January 1960). Ruabon to Llangollen trains were restored on 17th December 1964, but the entire route (except the part over Barmouth Bridge) was closed permanently a month later, on 18th January 1965. However, freight continued to Llangollen until 1968.

Llangollen Railway

The Llangollen Railway Society was formed in 1975 and a Light Railway Order to operate to Corwen was granted in 1984. A public service over a short distance from Llangollen began on 26th July 1981, using a push-pull system. Pentrefelin Loop was installed later, ¾ mile west of Llangollen, as a temporary reversal site and regular seasonal services began to Berwyn in March 1986. A loop was laid west of the station.

Extension of operation to Deeside Halt took place on 13th April 1990, with yet another temporary loop. Glyndyfrdwy was reached on 17th April 1992 and Carrog followed on 2nd May 1996.

Bala Lake Railway

Construction began in 1972 of a new line at 1ft 11⅝ins gauge, the Llanuwchllyn to Pentre Piod section being used from 13th August 1972, with trains running to Llangower from 15th September 1972. A further one mile to Pant-yr-hen-felin came into use in 1975 and the line to the end of the lake was opened on 27th March 1976.

PASSENGER SERVICES

The table on the right records the maximum number of down trains running on all sections of the route, at least five days per week. In the early years, one or two ran west as far as Corwen, while later on they terminated at Llangollen.

In the 20th century, there were extra trains between Dolgelley and Barmouth, some running inland to Drws-y-Nant. In the final two years, there were two trains from the east which ran to Bala Town only.

Additional trains for holiday traffic ran on Summer Saturdays from the mid-1940s to the early 1960s.

	Weekdays	Sundays
1869	5	1
1883	3	1
1912	5	0
1938	5	0
1948	5	0
1964	4	0

June 1869

June 1883

October 1912

RUABON, CORWEN, BALA, DOLGELLEY, and BARMOUTH.

Down. — Week Days.

Miles from Ruabon	Down.	mrn	mrn	mrn	mrn J	mrn	mrn	mrn J	mrn	mrn	mrn	aft	mrn	aft Z	mrn S	mrn
	Notes		Except Saturdays and School Holidays.			Mons. only.	Except Mondays		Fris. & Sats.					Except Saturdays and School Holidays.	TC London (Paddington) and Birkenhead to Pwllheli	TC London (Paddington) and Birkenhead to Pwllheli. Except Saturdays.
	108 London (Pad.) .. dep.	..	..	1 30	1 30	..	..	..	..	..	9R10	..	9R10	..	11R5	11R5
	108 Birmingham A. „	..	..	4*12	4*12	..	..	6 0	8 33	9 26	1115R		11R15	..	1R15	1R15
	108 Shrewsbury (Gen) „	..	..	5 35	5 35	..	..	7 45	10 0	11d50	1244	..	1 0		2 19	2 19
	112 Manchester B „	..	..	..	..	..	..	7 20	8 40	9 40	11 0	..	12 5		12 5	12 5
	112 Liverpool C ... „	..	..	..	6 15	..	..	8 0	9 30	9 50	1140	..	11B40		1 0	1 0
	112 Birkenhead (W) „	..	..	..	6 30	..	..	8 15	9 43	10 3	1155	..	11b55		1 18	1 18
	112 Chester (General) „	..	..	..	7 8	7 20	..	8 55	1018	11 5	1230	..	1 15		2 0	2 0
–	Ruabon .... dep.	..		7 0	7 43	8 25	..	9 35	11 0	12 47	1 15	..	2 1		3 5	3 5
1¼	Acrefair	..		7 5	7 48	8 30	..	9 40	11 4	12 51	1 19	..	2 5		..	..
2¼	Trevor	..		7 7	7 51	8 33	..	9 43	11 7	12 54	1 22	..	2 8		..	..
4½	Sun Bank Halt	..		..	..	8 38	..	..	..	..	..	..	..		..	..
6¼	Llangollen	..		7 14	8 0	8 42	..	9 50	1115	1 2	1 30	..	2 15		..	3 18
7¾	Berwyn	..		▬	8 5	m	..	9 55	▬	1 6	1 35	..	2 20		..	..
11¼	Glyndyfrdwy	..	8 5	Stop	8 15	▬	..	10 4	Stop	1 15	1 43	..	2 29		..	..
13½	Carrog ¶	..	8 10	..	8 19	Stop	..	10 9	..	1 20	1 48	..	2 35		..	..
16½	Corwen 514	..	8 15	..	8 27	..	..	1018	..	1 30	1 55	..	2 44		..	3 42
18½	Cynwyd	..	8 20	..	8 32			1022	..	m	2 0	..	m		..	Zz
21	Llandrillo	..	8 25	..	8 38			1028	..	▬	2 6	..	..	..	..	Zz
23¾	Llandderfel ¶	..	8 32	..	8 44			1034	..	Stop	2 12	..	..	..	..	Zz
28	Bala D (below) arr.	..	8 57	..	9 7			1055	..	..	2 21	..	..	..	..	4 12
	Bala dep.	..	..	..	8 50			1043	aft	..	..	..	..	3 40	..	3 40
32¼	Llanuwchllyn ¶	..	..	m	9 7	}	..	1057	m	..	..	..	..	3 59	..	Zz
38½	Drws-y-Nant ¶	..	..	8z30	9 21	mrn	..	1110	1 25	aft	..	..	..	W	..	Zz
42	Bontnewydd ¶	..	..	8z38	9 30	m	m	1120	1 33	m	..	..	..	..	..	Zz
45½	Dolgelley	7 0	..	8 50	9 40	1030	1040	1132	1 42	1 45	..	3 15	..	..	4 26	4 43
47½	Penmaenpool	7 5	..	8 54	9 48	1037	1047	1137		1 50	..	3 19	..	..	Zz	4 48
51¼	Arthog	718	..	9 6	10 0	1050	11 0	1150		2 2	..	3 32	..	..	..	5 1
52¾	Barmouth Junc. 146	721	..	9 10	10 4	1054	11 4	1153		2 6	..	3 36	..	..	4 46	5 5
54½	Barmouth .... arr.	727	..	9 15	1010	11 1	1110	1159		2 12	..	3 42	..	..	4 53	5 11
86½	146 Pwllheli ...... arr.	859	..	1055	..	..	..	1 43		3 59	..	5 45	..	..	6 10	6 30

Miles from Ruabon	Down.	mrn S J	aft	aft	mrn	aft	aft	aft J	aft	aft	aft	Sundays mrn		aft	aft	aft
	Notes		Except Saturdays. Runs Fridays only during School Holidays.	Road Motor Car.					Wednesdays and Saturdays.	Weds. & Sats. Road Motor Car.						
	108 London (Pad.) .. dep.	11R5		..	11R5	..	2R10	2R10	4R5		4R5	12L10	..	..	1R10	..
	108 Birmingham A. „	1R15		..	1R15	3R15	4R15	4R15	6R15		6R15	9 57	..	..	3R30	..
	108 Shrewsbury (Gen) „	2 19		..	2 19	4R27	5 30	5 30	7 28		7 28	11 17	..	..	5 10	6 0
	112 Manchester B „	12 5		..	1 45	1 45	3 38	4H30	6 40		6 40	11 50	..	..	3 25	..
	112 Liverpool C ... „	1 0		..	2 20	3 20	4 50	5 0	7 0		7 0	12 30	..	2 40	4 20	6 20
	112 Birkenhead (W) „	1 18		..	2 40	3 35	5 6	5 13	7 15		7 15	12 43	..	2 55	4 35	6 40
	112 Chester (General) „	2 0		..	3 15	4 20	5 10	5 55	8 0		8 0	1 20	..	3 40	5 30	7 30
–	Ruabon .... dep.	3 10			4 0	5 10	6 18	6 35	8 40		9 18	2V5	..	4V30	6V25	8V10
1¼	Acrefair	..			4 5	5 14	6 22	6 40	8 45		9 23	2V16	..	4V41	6V36	8V21
2¼	Trevor	..			4 7	5 17	6 25	6 43	8 49		9 26	2V23	..	4V48	6V43	8V28
4½	Sun Bank Halt	..			..	..	..	..	..	..	..	..	..	..	..	..
6¼	Llangollen	3 24			4 15	5 25	6 33	6 53	8 55	9 0	9 34	2V40	..	5V6	7V1	8V46
7¾	Berwyn	..			4 20	▬	..	6 58	m	9 8	..	2V48	..	..	7V9	8V54
11¼	Glyndyfrdwy	3 38			4 30	Stop	..	7 7		9 22	9 47	3V2	..	..	7V23	9V7
13½	Carrog ¶	Zz			4 35	..	..	7 12		9 30	9 51	3V13	..	..	7V34	9V16
16½	Corwen 514	3 50		4 10	4 47	..	..	7 21		9 40	10 0	3V25	..	..	7V45	9V26
18½	Cynwyd	Zz		4 18	4 52	..	..	7 26		..	10 4	..	..	..	..	..
21	Llandrillo	Zz		4 30	4 58	..	..	7 32		..	1010	..	..	..	..	..
23¾	Llandderfel ¶	Zz		4 42	5 4	..	..	7 38		..	1016	..	..	..	..	..
28	Bala D (below) arr.	4 20		..	5 13	..	..	7 55		..	1026	..	..	..	..	..
	Bala dep.	4 5	..	5 0	..	..	..	7 40		..	..	..	..	..	..	..
32¼	Llanuwchllyn ¶	4 24	m	5 22	..	..	..	7 59		..	..	..	..	..	..	..
38½	Drws-y-Nant ¶	4 36	5 10	5 43	..	aft	..	8 20		..	..	..	..	..	..	..
42	Bontnewydd ¶	4 45	5 18	5 57	..	m	..	8 28		..	..	..	..	..	..	..
45½	Dolgelley	4 55	5 27	6 10	..	6 25	..	8 38		..	..	..	..	..	..	..
47½	Penmaenpool	5 0	..	..	..	6 30	..	8 43		..	..	..	..	..	..	..
51¼	Arthog	5 13	..	..	..	6 43	..	8 56		..	..	..	..	..	..	..
52¾	Barmouth Junc. 146	5 17	..	..	..	6 48	..	8 59		..	..	..	..	..	..	..
54½	Barmouth .... arr.	5 23	..	..	..	6 54	..	9 5	..	..	..	..	..	..	..	..
86½	146 Pwllheli ...... arr.	7 8	..	..	..	8 40	..	..	..	..	..	..	..	..	..	..

A Snow Hill. **B** Exchange Sta. B Dep. 12 20 aft. Sats. *b* Dep. 12 33 aft. Sats. **C** Landing Stage. **D** Passengers to and from Bala change at Bala Jn. by most of the trains. *d* Dep. 11 40 mrn. Sats. **E** or E Except Sats. H 10 mins. later Sats. **J** Stops at **Flag Station** between Llandderfel and Llanuwchllyn, and at Garneddwen Halt between Llanuwchllyn & Drws-y-Nant when required. Passengers wishing to alight must inform Guard at previous *stopping* sta. L Sat. night. **m** One class only. R Restaurant Car Train. **S** or S Sats. only **TC** Thro Carriage. V Road Motor Car. **W** Runs to Garneddwen Halt, arriving 4 9 aft. Zz Stops set down from beyond Ruabon on informing Guard at Ruabon. **Z** Calls at **Flag Station** when required. z Except Sats. & School Holidays. * 5 mins. later on Mons. ¶ "Halts" at Bonwm, between Carrog and Corwen, at Llangower, between Llandderfel and Llanuwchllyn, at Llys between Llanuwchllyn and Drws-y-Nant, at Wnion, between Drws-y-Nant & Bontnewydd & at Dolserau between Bontnewydd & Dolgelley.

March 1938

Table 187 RUABON, CORWEN, BALA, DOLGELLEY, and BARMOUTH

Week Days only

Ruabon	ngt	a.m	a.m	a.m	a.m	a.m S	a.m E	a.m S	p.m	a.m S	a.m	a.m	a.m	p.m	a.m	p.m	p.m	p.m	p.m E	p.m S
Notes		Except Saturdays and School Holidays								TC London (Paddington) to Pwllheli				Except Saturdays and School Holidays						
153 London (Pad.) .... dep	12 5	..	..	..	..	..	..	..	..	9 0	9S 0	9Y10	11R10	..	11R10	..	..	2 10	4Y10	4Y10
153 Birmingham A .. „	4 10	..	..	..	..	6 0	6 0	8 22	..	1120	8P36	11Y56	1R43	..	1R43	..	2H55	4 45	6Y52	6Y52
153 Shrewsbury ..... „	5 46	..	..	..	..	7 40	7 40	9 45	..	1230	10P45	1 10	2R58	..	2R58	..	4 15	6 0	8 5	8 5
153 Manchester (Ex.) „	10B20	..	..	..	..	6 5	6 5	8 35	..	10 0	10E25	11 45	..	..	1 35	..	..	4 30	5 35	5 35
153 Birkenhead (W.) „	11B10	..	..	..	6 30	7 43	7 50	9 20	..	1140	11 40	12L25	1 10	..	2 35	..	3Z13	5 5	7 12	7 12
153 Chester .... „	12F20	..	..	..	7 15	8 28	8 40	10 0	..	1222	12 22	1 17	1 50	..	3 17	..	4 20	5 50	7 55	7 55
Ruabon .... dep	7 0	..	..	7 15	8 25	9 18	9 31	11 0	..	1 13	1 20	2 10	3 45	..	4 0	..	5 7	7 0	9 34	9 59
Acrefair	7 5	..	..	7 21	8 30	9 23	9 36	..	..		1 26	2 16	..	..	4 5	..	5 12	7 6	9 39	10 4
Trevor	7 8	..	..	7 25	8 33	9 26	9 39	..	..		1 29	2 19	..	..	4 8	..	5 15	7 10	9 42	10 7
Sun Bank Halt	..	..	..	..	8 38	..	..	..	..		..	..	..	..	..	..	..	..	..	..
Llangollen	7 15		..	7 35	8 42	9 35	9 48	11 17	..		1 38	2 30	3 58		4 16	..	5 22	7 20	9 50	1015
Berwyn	..		..	7 40	(3)	9 40	9 53	..	..		1 46	2 35	..		4 25	..	..	7 26	Dd	Dd
Glyndyfrdwy	..		..	7 49	..	9 53	10 2	..	..		1 55	2 42	..		4 35	..	..	7 35	10 3	1028
Carrog	..		..	7 55	..	9 58	10 7	..	..		2 0	2 47	..		4 41	..	..	7 40	10 9	1034
Bonwm Halt	..		..	..	..	..	..	..	..		2 4	..	..		4 45	..	..	7 44	..	..
Corwen	..		..	8 5	..	10 7	10 15	11 45	..		2 10	2 55	4 20		4 53	..	..	7 50	1015	1040
Cynwyd	..		..	8 10	..	10 12	10 20	..	..		2 15	3 0	..		5 0	..	..	7 55	1020	1045
Llandrillo	..		..	8 17	..	10 21	10 25	..	..		2 20	3 6	..		5 5	..	..	8 0	1025	1050
Llandderfel	..		..	8 23	..	10 28	10 32	..	..		2 26	3 12	..		5 11	..	..	8 6	1031	1056
Bala D ...... arr	..		..	8 45	..	10 55	10 55	12 22	..		2 36	3 39	4 50		5 21	..	..	8 27	1041	11 6
Bala dep	..		..	8 30	..	10 30	10 30	12 6	..		(3)	3 15	4 30		..	..	..	8 5	..	..
Llangower Halt	..		..	8 42	..	10 47	10 47	..	..	..	..	3 27	..		..	..	..	8 19	..	..
Flag Station Halt	..		..	8 46	..	..	..	..	..	..	..	3 31	..		..	..	..	8 23	..	..
Llanuwchllyn	..		..	8 51	..	10 56	10 56	..	..	..	..	3 38	Dd		..	..	..	8 29	..	..
Llys Halt	..		..	8 56	..	10 58	10 58	..	..	..	..	3 43	..		..	..	..	8 34	..	..
Garneddwen Halt	..	(3)	..	Nn	..	Nn	Nn	..	..	..	..	3 48	..	(3)	..	..	..	Nn	..	..
Drws-y-nant	..	8 0	..	9 8	..	11 15	11 15	..	..	..	..	3 55	Dd	5 15	..	..	..	8 46	..	..
Wnion Halt	..	8 5	..	9 12	..	11 20	11 20	..	..	..	..	4 0	..	5 20	..	..	..	8 51	..	..
Bontnewydd	..	8 10	..	9 18	..	11 25	11 25	..	..	..	..	4 5	Dd	5 24	..	..	..	8 56	..	..
Dolserau Halt	..	8 15	(3)	9 22	..	..	..	..	(3)	..	..	..	..	5 28	..	(3)	..	..	..	..
Dolgelley	..	8 19	8 30	9‡31	..	11†39	11†39	12†55	1 45	..	..	4†17	5 21	5 32	..	6 18	..	9 6	..	..
Penmaenpool	..	..	8 35	9 45	..	11 44	11 44	..	1 50	..	..	4 22	Dd	..	..	6 23	..	9 12	..	..
Arthog	..	..	8 48	9 58	..	11 57	11 57	..	2 3	..	..	4 35	..	..	..	6 36	..	9 25	..	..
Barmouth Junc.	..	..	8 51	10 2	..	12 0	12 0	1 15	2 6	..	..	4 38	5 39	..	..	6 39	..	9 29	..	..
Barmouth .... arr	..	..	8 57	10 8	..	12 8	12 8	1 24	2 12	3 25	..	4 45	5 45	..	..	6 45	..	9 35	..	..
189 Pwllheli .... arr	..	..	1055	..	..	2 1	2 1	2 58	4 10	4 59	..	6 22	7T11	..	..	9 45	..	..	..	..

A Snow Hill
B Except Sunday nights
D Passengers to and from Bala change at Bala Junc. by most of the Trains
Dd Calls to set down from beyond Ruabon on informing Guard at Ruabon
E or E Except Saturdays
F Except Monday mornings
H Fridays and Saturdays
L Dep. 12 30 p.m on Saturdays

Nn Calls to take up or set down passengers. Passengers wishing to alight must give notice to the Guard at previous *stopping* Station and those desiring to join should give the necessary hand signal to the Driver.
P Dep. Birmingham 11 20 a.m. and Shrewsbury 12 30 p.m. on Sats.
R Restaurant Car Train
S or S Saturdays only

T Arr. 7 18 p.m. on Saturdays
TC Through Carriages
V Restaurant Car to Shrewsbury
Y Buffet Car to Wolverhampton
Z Dep. 3 30 p.m. on Saturdays
† Arr. 5 mins. *earlier*
‡ Arr. 4 mins. *earlier*
(3) Third class only

May 1948

June 1961

Table 187 RUABON, CORWEN, BALA, DOLGELLAU and BARMOUTH

WEEK DAYS ONLY

Ruabon	am	am	am	am	am	am		pm	am	am	noon	am	am	am		pm	pm	pm	pm	pm	
Notes	Saturdays only	Except Saturdays and School Holidays	Except Saturdays			Saturdays only			TC Birmingham (Snow Hill) to Barmouth and Pwllheli. Saturdays only. Will not run after 26th August	Saturdays only. Will not run after 2nd September. TC London (Paddington) to Pwllheli. RC London (Paddington) to Barmouth		Saturdays only	Except Sats.	Sats. only		Except Saturdays and School Holidays					
152 London (Paddington) .. dep	..	..	..	12 5	..	..	..	..	..	9 0	..	9 10	11 10	11 10	..	..	..	..	2 10	4 10	..
152 Birmingham (Snow Hill) .. „	..	..	..	4 0	6 0	8 32	..	..	11 0	11 20	..	11 46	1 26	1 42	..	..	..	..	4 21	6B40	..
152 Wolverhampton (L.L.) .. „	..	..	..	4 30	6 25	9 3	..	..	11 34	11 48	..	12 14	1 53	2 9	..	..	..	..	4 53	7B10	..
152 Shrewsbury .. „	..	..	..	5 35	7 35	9 50	..	..	..	12 31	12E 0	1 4	2 40	2 55	..	..	..	..	5 40	8B 3	..
Manchester (Exchange) .. „	..	..	..	..	..	8 30	..	..	10 25	10 25	10 25	11 37	11 55	11 55	..	..	1Y45	..	4 30	5 35	..
152 Birkenhead (Woodside) .. „	..	..	..	..	7 50	9 30	..	..	11 40	11 40	11 40	12 25	1 25	1 12	..	..	2 35	..	5 7	7 13	..
152 Chester (General) „	..	..	..	..	8 45	10 10	..	..	12 22	12 22	12 22	1 20	2 2	1 50	..	..	3 15	..	5 55	7 55	..
Ruabon .. dep	..		..	7 17	9 27	11 0	..	..	1 0	1 13	1 21	2 0	3 28	3 42	..		4 0	..	6 45	9 34	..
Acrefair	..		..	7 23	9 32	..	..	..		..	1 25	2 6	..	..	..		4 4	..	6 50	9 38	..
Trevor	..		..	..	9 35	..	..	..		..	1 28	2 9	..	..	..		4 7	..	6 54	9 41	..
Llangollen	..		..	7 37	9 45	11 16	..	..		..	1 38	2 18	3 43	3 58	..		4 16	..	7 5	9 50	..
Berwyn Halt	..		..	7 42	9 50	..	..	..		..	1 45	2 23			..		4 25	..	7 12	dd	..
Glyndyfrdwy	..		..	7 54	9 59	..	..	..		..	1 54	2 31			..		4 35	..	7 20	10 3	..
Carrog	..		..	7 58	10 4	..	..	..		..	1 59	2 36			..		4 41	..	7 25	10 8	..
Bonwm Halt	..		..	..	..	..	..	..		..	2 3	..	..	..	..		4 45	..	..	..	..
Corwen	..		..	8 9	10 14	11 40	..	..		..	2 10	2 46	4 5	4 21	..		4 53	..	7 34	10 15	..
Cynwyd	..		..	8 14	10 19	..	..	..		..	2 14	2 50	..	..	..		4 59	..	7 39	10 19	..
Llandrillo	..		..	8 20	10 25	..	..	..		..	2 20	2 56	..	..	..		5 5	..	7 45	10 25	..
Llandderfel	..		..	8 26	10 31	..	..	..		..	2 26	3 2	..	..	..		5 11	..	7 51	10 31	..
Bala G .. arr	..	..	..	8 45	10 55	12 17	..	..		..	2 36	3 22	4 32	4 50	..	..	5 21	..	8 12	10 41	..
Bala dep	..	..	..	8 30	10 30	12 0	..	..		..	(2)	3 5	4 17	4 30	..	..	..	..	7 50	..	..
Llangower Halt		..		8 42	10 47		..	..			..	3 15	4 32	..	..	..	..	..	8 4	..	..
Glan Llyn Halt		..		8 46	10S51		..	..			..	3 19	..	..	..	..	..	..	8 8	..	..
Llanuwchllyn		..		8 51	10 57		..	..			..	3 25	4 38	dd	..	..	..	..	8 19	..	..
Llys Halt		..		8 56	11 0		..	..			..	3 29	..	..	..	..	..	..	8 24	..	..
Garneddwen Halt		(2)		nn	nn		..	..			..	3 35	..	..	..	(2)	..	..	nn	..	..
Drws-y-Nant		8 5		9 8	11 20		..	..			..	3 42	dd	dd	..	5 0	..	..	8 36	..	..
Wnion Halt		8 10		9 12	11 23		..	..			..	3 46	..	..	..	5 4	..	..	8 41	..	..
Bontnewydd		8 14		9 18	11 30	..	..	..			..	3 52	4 58	dd	..	5 8	..	..	8 46	..	..
Dolgellau arr	(2)	8 21	(2)	9 26	11 37	12 50	..	(2)	2 40		..	3 59	5 5	5 19	..	5 15	..	(2)	8 53	..	..
Dolgellau dep	8 20	..	8 30	9 31	11 38	12 54	..	1 41	2 44	..	..	4 2	5 8	5 20	..	..	..	6 20	8 56	..	..
Penmaenpool	8 24	..	8 34	9 46	11 43	..	..	1 45	..	..	..	4 6	5 13	dd	..	..	..	6 24	9 0	..	..
Arthog	8 37	..	8 47	9 58	11 56	..	..	1 58	..	..	..	4 19	5 27	dd	..	..	..	6 37	9 13	..	..
Morfa Mawddach	8 42	..	8 52	10 4	12X 6	1 19	..	2b 5	..	3 22	..	4 25	5 33	5 46	..	..	..	6 43	9 18	..	..
Barmouth arr	8 47	..	8 57	10 10	12X11	1 24	..	2 10	3 16	3 28	..	4 30	5 33	5 51	..	..	..	6 48	9 23	..	..
189 Pwllheli arr	1057	..	10 57	12S 0	1 55	2 50	..	4 0	4 30	4 50	..	6 12	7 7	7 38	..	..	..	8H37	..	..	..

B On Saturdays dep Birmingham (Snow Hill) 6 48 pm, Wolverhampton (L.L.) 7 18 and Shrewsbury 8 7 pm
b Arrives 3 minutes *earlier*
dd Calls to set down from beyond Ruabon on notice being given to the Guard at Ruabon
E Except Saturdays
G Passengers to and from Bala change at Bala Junc. by most of the trains
H On Saturdays arr 8 47 pm
nn Calls to take up or set down passengers during hours of daylight only. Passengers wishing to alight must give notice to the Guard at previous *stopping* station and those desiring to join should give the necessary hand signal to the Driver
RC Restaurant Car
S Saturdays only
TC Through Carriages
Y On Saturdays dep 1 55 pm
X On Mondays to Fridays runs 4 minutes later

(2) Second class only

RUABON

II.　　This 1914 survey at 6ins to 1mile has Ruabon station top right and the main line mainly on the right page. The first two stations on the Llangollen line are on the left page, as is the southern part of the single-track Pont Cysyllte branch. This was opened in 1863 by the Shropshire Union Railways & Canal Company, ↘

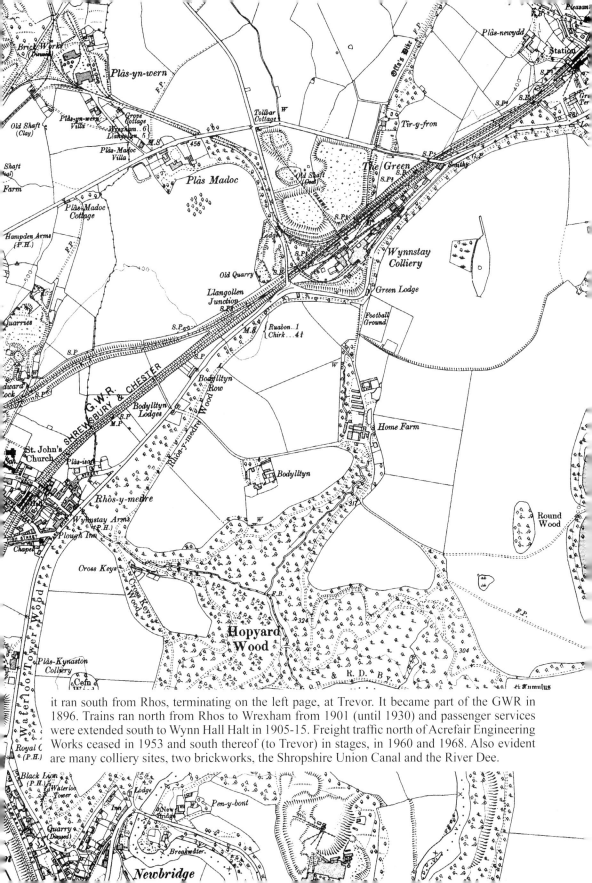

it ran south from Rhos, terminating on the left page, at Trevor. It became part of the GWR in 1896. Trains ran north from Rhos to Wrexham from 1901 (until 1930) and passenger services were extended south to Wynn Hall Halt in 1905-15. Freight traffic north of Acrefair Engineering Works ceased in 1953 and south thereof (to Trevor) in stages, in 1960 and 1968. Also evident are many colliery sites, two brickworks, the Shropshire Union Canal and the River Dee.

1.   A southward panorama from the mid-1950s includes a siding curving on the right to the 65ft turntable and also Middle Box, which had 59 levers and was in use until 4th June 1987. North Box had 31 and lasted until 26th September 1965. (Lens of Sutton coll.)

2.   "Dukedog" nos 9017 and 9014 are about to start their journey to Minffordd with the Festiniog Railway Society's AGM Special on 26th April 1958. The train was hauled here from London by record breaking 4-4-0 no. 3440 *City of Truro*. (M.J.Stretton coll.)

3.   Heading the 5.10pm Ruabon to Pwllheli on 8th August 1965 is 4-6-0 no. 75027. Many trains for the Llangollen line started from this bay platform. The left half of the footbridge gave the station master and the occupant of Plas Newydd access to their dwellings. (D.A.Johnson)

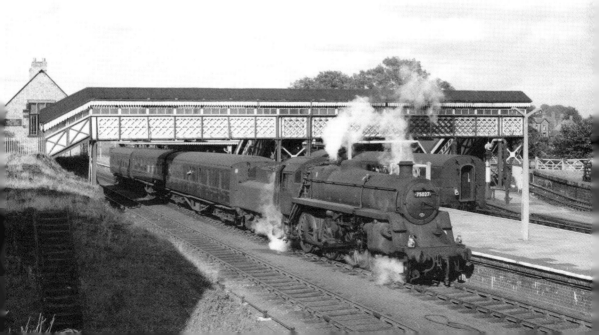

4.   The goods yard is seen in the Summer of 1964; it closed on 7th December of that year. Behind the camera was South Box, which had a 54-lever frame and was in use until 18th May 1969. Back in 1947, a shunting engine was available for 20 hours in every 24. The tank contained 37,000 gallons of water and supplied five columns. (P.J.Garland/R.S.Carpenter)

Other views of this area can be seen in our *Shrewsbury to Chester* album.

5.   Staffing ceased in February 1974 and the building later became offices. It is seen on 28th April 2001 as the Mid-Hants Railway's Crompton no. D6593 runs in with the return Chester-Alton railtour. The passengers seen had visited the Llangollen Railway. (P.G.Barnes)

LLANGOLLEN LINE JUNCTION

6.   The location is indicated near the centre of the right page of map II, but it does not show the full name. This 1962 panorama has our route on the right and the line to Shrewsbury straight on. There had been a signal box below the camera from 1884 to 1933; it had 27 levers, when closed. (P.J.Garland/R.S.Carpenter)

3rd-SINGLE   SINGLE-3rd
8636   8636
Ruabon to
Ruabon   Ruabon
5.00   8.00
Acrefair Johnstown & H   Acrefair Johnstown & H
or Rhosymedre Halt   or Rhosymedre Halt
ACREFAIR   JOHNSTOWN & HAFOD
or RHOSYMEDRE HALT
(W)   2d. H   FARE   2d. H   (W)
For Conditions see over   For Conditions see over

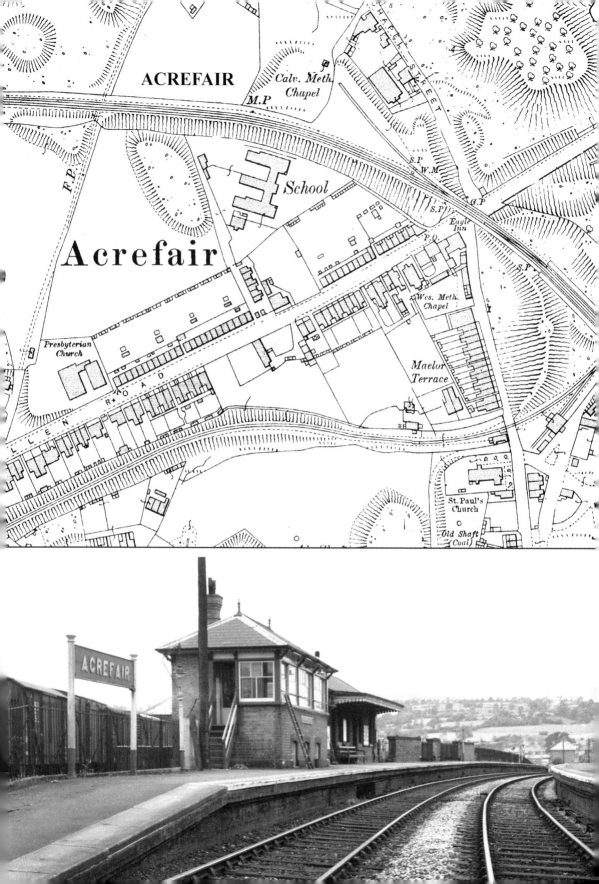

ACREFAIR

Calv. Meth. Chapel

M.P

School

Acrefair

Presbyterian Church

Eagle Inn

P.O.

Wes. Meth. Chapel

Maelor Terrace

St. Paul's Church

Old Shaft (Coal)

ACREFAIR

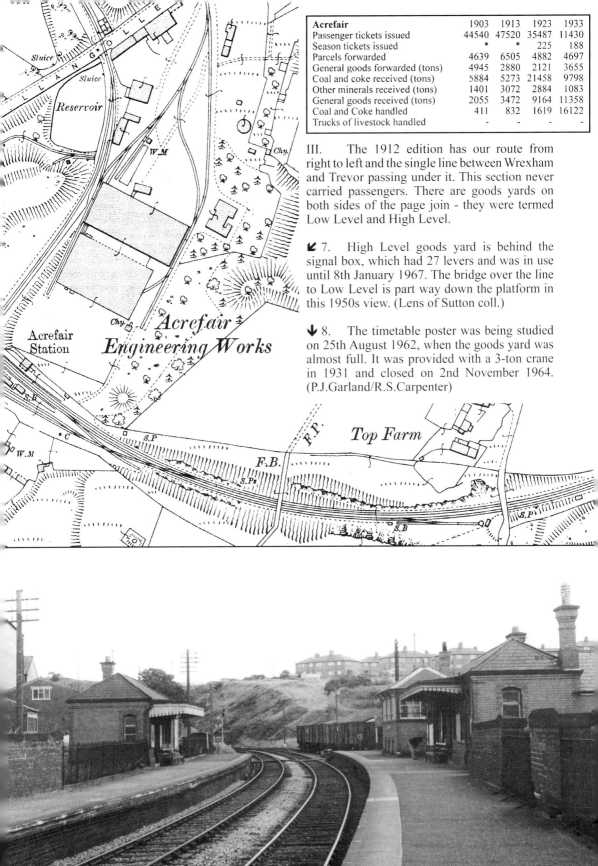

Acrefair	1903	1913	1923	1933
Passenger tickets issued	44540	47520	35487	11430
Season tickets issued	*	*	225	188
Parcels forwarded	4639	6505	4882	4697
General goods forwarded (tons)	4945	2880	2121	3655
Coal and coke received (tons)	5884	5273	21458	9798
Other minerals received (tons)	1401	3072	2884	1083
General goods received (tons)	2055	3472	9164	11358
Coal and Coke handled	411	832	1619	16122
Trucks of livestock handled	-	-	-	-

III. The 1912 edition has our route from right to left and the single line between Wrexham and Trevor passing under it. This section never carried passengers. There are goods yards on both sides of the page join - they were termed Low Level and High Level.

↙ 7. High Level goods yard is behind the signal box, which had 27 levers and was in use until 8th January 1967. The bridge over the line to Low Level is part way down the platform in this 1950s view. (Lens of Sutton coll.)

↓ 8. The timetable poster was being studied on 25th August 1962, when the goods yard was almost full. It was provided with a 3-ton crane in 1931 and closed on 2nd November 1964. (P.J.Garland/R.S.Carpenter)

9.   Low Level Yard was photographed from the platform on the same day. From 1923 to 1938, nine men diminishing to seven were provided for the station and both yards. The station had been called "Cefn Mawr" in its first few months. St. Paul's Church and the gasworks are included, but the coal mine had closed. (P.J.Garland/R.S.Carpenter)

Gt Western Ry   Gt Western Ry
ACREFAIR   ACREFAIR
496   TO   496
TREVOR
THIRD CLASS
2d N Fare 2d N
Issued subject to the conditions & regulations as
set in the Company's Time Tables Bills & Notices.
Trevor   Trevor

Gt Western Ry   Gt Western Ry
RUABON   RUABON
1323   TO   1323
TREVOR
THIRD CLASS
2½d C Fare 2½d C
Trevor   Trevor
FOR CONDITIONS SEE BACK.(W.L

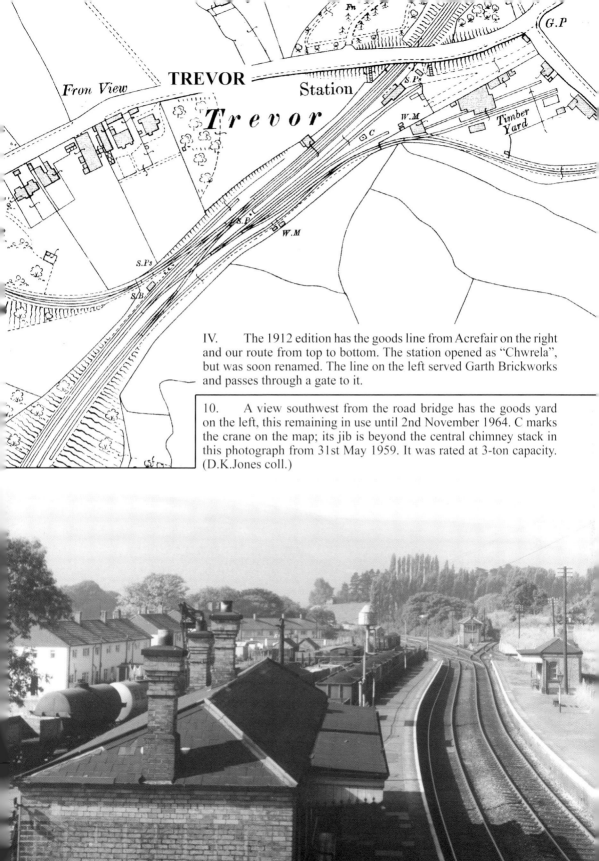

TREVOR Station

Trevor

Fron View

G.P

Timber Yard

IV.   The 1912 edition has the goods line from Acrefair on the right and our route from top to bottom. The station opened as "Chwrela", but was soon renamed. The line on the left served Garth Brickworks and passes through a gate to it.

10.   A view southwest from the road bridge has the goods yard on the left, this remaining in use until 2nd November 1964. C marks the crane on the map; its jib is beyond the central chimney stack in this photograph from 31st May 1959. It was rated at 3-ton capacity. (D.K.Jones coll.)

11.   As at Acrefair, the GWR buildings dated from around 1900, when the track doubling took place. Cuttings and embankments seem to alternate on this section of the route, which is down at 1 in 85 towards Llangollen in this vicinity. (Lens of Sutton coll.)

Trevor	1903	1913	1923	1933
Passenger tickets issued	31636	28440	29049	10342
Season tickets issued	*	*	264	175
Parcels forwarded	4695	5563	2728	2785
General goods forwarded (tons)	7540	5981	4210	2452
Coal and coke received (tons)	17202	9272	4589	3515
Other minerals received (tons)	4035	8966	12305	8986
General goods received (tons)	2159	1612	767	351
Coal and Coke handled	-	3366	6259	5220
Trucks of livestock handled	-	-	-	-

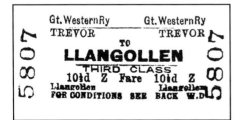

12.   The goods line from the north is lower left and a pick-up goods train from Llangollen is seen sometime between 1965 and 1967. The signal box had a 32-lever frame and closed on 13th November 1967. About one mile west was Wright's siding. It was used for limestone until the mid-1930s. (Dr G.B.Sutton)

SUN BANK HALT

13.   On the morning of 9th September 1945, a breach occurred in the bank of the Shropshire Union Canal's Llangollen branch. The torrent tore away the embankment of the line below and the 3.35am Chester-Barmouth mail and goods train, plunged into the void. The engine was 2-6-0 no. 6315. The short goods train piled on top of it and caught fire; the driver was killed and the engine was cut up on site. (GWR)

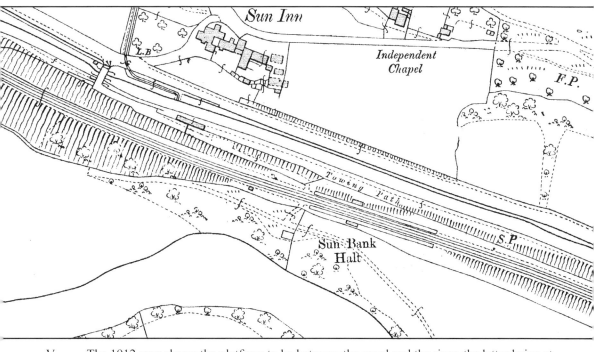

V. The 1912 map shows the platform to be between the canal and the river, the latter being at the lowest level. The halt opened on 24th July 1905 and was called "Garth & Sun Bank" until 1st July 1906.

14. The halt closed on 5th June 1950 and the site was photographed in about 1959, as a 5700 class 0-6-0PT, was passing by. The 1949 timetable showed an 8.38am to Llangollen only and no up service. (J.W.T.House/C.L.Caddy coll.)

VI.   The 1912 map has three tracks at the top left. The one on the right was the goods yard headshunt and it extended to Pentrefelin sidings, described in caption 26. The double track ended near them, at Llangollen Goods Junction. The crane in the goods yard had a 3-ton capacity. Sample staffing levels were 1903-20, 1913-17 and 1933-13. W.M. indicates a weighing machine for carts.

Llangollen	1903	1913	1923	1933
Passenger tickets issued	88184	71637	67554	21720
Season tickets issued	*	*	329	577
Parcels forwarded	33294	31420	30092	24199
General goods forwarded (tons)	2215	2048	1185	1087
Coal and coke received (tons)	7322	7166	6782	2881
Other minerals received (tons)	3950	1966	1793	1423
General goods received (tons)	4590	4113	4300	2060
Coal and Coke handled	127	186	304	2971
Trucks of livestock handled	313	334	310	54

School

Siambr-wen

Station   S.P   L.B

P.H

W.M

S.P

S.P

Llangollen
Bridge

Towing Pa

Ponsonby Arms
(P.H.)

MILL STREET

Corn Mill

Weir

Royal
Hotel

Sluice   F.B.

Weir

Overflow   F.B

F.B.

Bowling
Green

Club

PARADE STREET

Fn

BANK

School

Pol. Sta.

Chapel

P.O

BRIDGE STREET

P.H.

P.H

Dee Mill
(Flannel)

Congregational
Chapel

EAST STREET

GREENFIELD

CASTLE STREET

OAK STREET

CHAPEL STREET

Hand
Hotel

St. Collen's
Church
(Vicarage)

CHURCH STREET

SMITHFIELD

Zion Chapel
(Wes. Meth.)

W.M

Grave Yard
S.D

Chapel

15.   An upstream panorama emphasises the proximity of the River Dee to the line. When it was doubled around 1900, the GWR had to encroach upon the river bed. The postcard includes the short station approach road. (M.Dart coll.)

16.   A view in the same direction from the road bridge in 1957 features ex-GWR 2-6-0 no. 5322 with a train from the coast. The station entrance is hidden by the signal box, but a lorry shows the position of the access road. (J.W.T.House/C.L.Caddy coll.)

17.	The west end was known as the "Excursion Platforms" and they had ramps to a minor road. However, the platforms were continuous. Nos 4375 and 6344 run in with the 8.45am from Pwllheli on 15th August 1953. Both were 2-6-0s. Excursions were often run from Liverpool, with two appearing on some Sundays. (H.C.Casserley)

18.	The dock on the right was termed the "Horse Landing", many early wealthy passengers taking their horses with them. Piloting a "Manor" class 4-6-0 in the early 1950s is 0-6-0PT no. 9669. In the distance are the two separate waiting rooms for the excursion platforms. (M.Whitehouse coll.)

19.   We look east from the road bridge in 1957 and see 2-6-0 no. 6357 passing the short up siding. The Dee could be enjoyed for many miles of train travel to come. (J.W.T.House/C.L.Caddy coll.)

20.   Goods traffic continued as far as Llangollen until 1st April 1968 and this is the view on 28th June of that year. The Flint & Deeside Railway Preservation Society was formed in 1972 and it later leased the station, together with three miles of route. (C.L.Caddy)

21.   The signal box had 25 levers and was in use until 18th January 1967. It was often switched out as Llangollen Goods Junction had greater importance, being at the end of the double track. This sad view is included to show that all structures survived, including the excursion buildings in the distance. (D.K.Jones)

22.   Seen in about 1976, the station was the subject of a restoration scheme and it was opened to the public on 13th September 1975. By 1982, ¾ mile of track had been laid towards Corwen. The signal box returned to use on 3rd May 1991, enabling two trains to pass here and at Llangollen Goods Junction. (M.J.Stretton coll.)

23.   The double curves are evident as no. 7822 *Foxcote Manor* waits to depart on 10th April 1988, within one week of its return to traffic. The canopies are on the former excursion waiting rooms and are devoid of stanchions. (H.Ballantyne)

WEST OF LLANGOLLEN

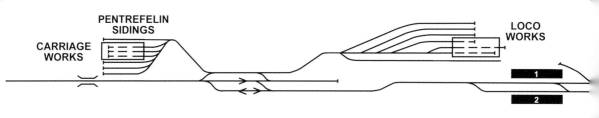

VII.   The goods yard once had four sidings to hold 108 wagons and, further west, another four to contain 188. However, three of these were usually kept for excursion stock. One continued to a canal wharf, where slate was transhipped.

24.   Use of the former goods shed was possible from May 1981, after it was vacated by a seed merchant. It was extended, as seen on 28th June 2008, for locomotive purposes. No. 44806 was built by the LMS in 1944 and carries the name *Kenneth Aldcroft*. The goods shed had two one-ton cranes and there was a 3-ton one in the yard. (V.Mitchell)

25.   Part of the base of the Llangollen Goods Junction box had remained, but the frame came from Ruabon Middle and much of the timber part from Green Lane, Saltney. It is seen on 17th June 1989, a few weeks after commissioning, in the company of no. 7822 *Foxcote Manor*, which is westbound with a demonstration freight train. (T.Heavyside)

26.   Pentrefelin sidings were relaid in 1981 and are seen from a westbound train climbing towards the viaduct on 28th June 2008. The new and spacious storage shed is in the background. (V.Mitchell)

27.   Few enjoy the majesty of this remarkable location, but we can gasp at the sight of ex-LMS class 3F 0-6-0T rumbling over the structure on 20th March 1993. (T.Heavyside)

→ 28. The bridge over the River Dee was supporting 4-6-0 no. 7822 *Foxcote Manor* on 6th May 1991, as it hauled the 13.15 Llangollen to Deeside Halt service. It was built in 1950 and stood in Barry scrapyard from 1965 until 1974. Extensive bridge repairs had been undertaken in 1984-85. (T.Heavyside)

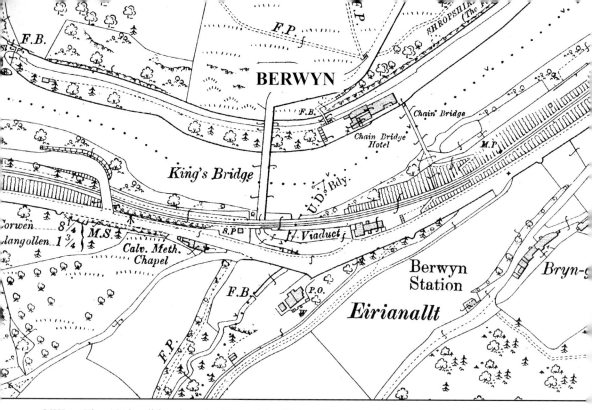

VIII.   The 1912 edition has the Shropshire Union Canal running north of the River Dee and branching south from this is a stream which traverses a deep ravine.

Berwyn	1903	1913	1923	1933
Passenger tickets issued	14710	11450	1471	5819
Season tickets issued	*	27	61	42
Parcels forwarded	1471	1933	1661	750

29.   This eastward panorama includes the chain bridge and the roof of the hotel of that name, both of which can be found on the map. (HMRS)

30.   The suffix HALT was added in 1954, after staffing ceased and not long before this record was made. There had been just one man listed here from 1913 on and he had a distinctly impressive residence. (Lens of Sutton coll.)

31.   BR class 4 2-6-0 no. 76026 arrives with the 07.10 from Barmouth on 7th November 1964. The term HALT was not used after the station was reopened. (E.Wilmshurst)

32.   The 3.0pm from Llangollen was hauled by 0-4-2T no. 1466 on 7th September 1986. It was on loan from the Great Western Society at Didcot. This section of the route was reopened to passengers in March 1986. The viaduct is 77yds in length and further west is Berwyn Tunnel, which is 689yds long. The A5 passes over this twice. (H.Ballantyne)

33. The road bridge over the river is in the background, as *Burtonwood Brewer* arrives on 30th August 1986. It was an 0-6-0ST built by Kitson in 1932. Its original name of *Austin 1* was restored in 1992. A run-round loop was in use in 1986-90 and it was situated beyond the road bridge over the line, west of the station. (T.Heavyside)

DEESIDE HALT

34.   Traffic commenced at the 3-coach platform on 13th April 1990. The GWR had a passing loop in this vicinity. Its signal box had an 18-lever frame and was in use from 1908 until 1964. (B.Dobbs)

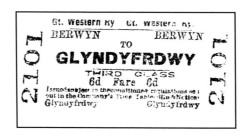

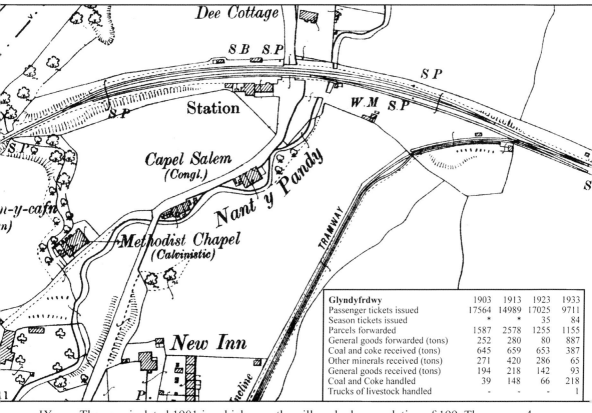

Glyndyfrdwy	1903	1913	1923	1933
Passenger tickets issued	17564	14989	17025	9711
Season tickets issued	*	*	35	84
Parcels forwarded	1587	2578	1255	1155
General goods forwarded (tons)	252	280	80	887
Coal and coke received (tons)	645	659	653	387
Other minerals received (tons)	271	420	286	65
General goods received (tons)	194	218	142	93
Coal and Coke handled	39	148	66	218
Trucks of livestock handled	-	-	-	1

IX.   The map is dated 1901 in which year the village had a population of 199. There were 4 or 5 employees here in 1929-38. The tramway conveyed slate from Moelferna Quarry to an exchange platform. North of it is the small goods yard, with sidings for 8 and 13 wagons.

35.   An unusual subject for a postcard was an up goods train being shunted. There is a loading gantry over one of the sidings for slate transhipment. (R.S.Carpenter coll.)

36.   The main building had local stone, whereas the up shelter comprised red Ruabon bricks. There was a 13-lever signal box in 1877-97, but this subsequent one had 25. The date is 25th August 1962. (P.J.Garland/R.S.Carpenter)

37.   Reopening took place on 17th April 1992 and 0-6-0 no. 2392 was recorded on 5th July of that year. It was on loan from the North Yorkshire Moors Railway. Restoration work involved providing a fresh signal box; it came from Leaton and can be found in our *Shrewsbury to Chester* album. (T.Heavyside)

38.   Two views from 10th September 1995 complete our survey. The up side building was replaced with a timber structure and a footbridge was required, as were picnic tables. No. 7822 *Foxcote Manor* is seen again. (E.Wilmshurst)

39.   The fine station house survived, but the platforms had to be raised. A siding was laid on the north side of the line, instead of the south, but the resulting atmosphere is magnificent. (E.Wilmshurst)

CARROG

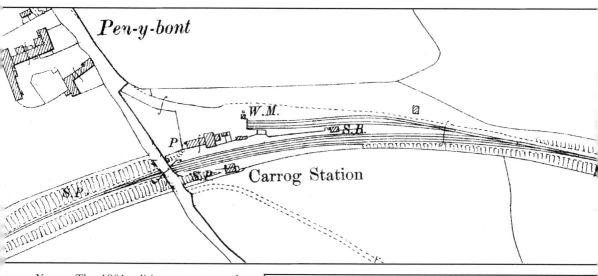

X. The 1901 edition came out when the parishioners numbered 192. There was a staff of three in the 1913-38 period.

40. Few changes took place, a notable exception being the application of electric lights to the old posts and the arrival of a camping coach in some Summers in the 1950s. (M.J.Stretton coll.)

Carrog	1903	1913	1923	1933
Passenger tickets issued	13869	12097	14044	9200
Season tickets issued	*	*	33	63
Parcels forwarded	2928	2836	1504	1543
General goods forwarded (tons)	53	74	62	525
Coal and coke received (tons)	805	723	563	177
Other minerals received (tons)	133	334	327	42
General goods received (tons)	510	406	246	74
Coal and Coke handled	47	103	348	538
Trucks of livestock handled	7	36	9	13

41.   The westward view in June 1968 changed little until work started on renovation in the 1990s. The signal box was in use from 1897 until 1964 and had a 19-lever frame. (C.L.Caddy)

42.   The station was reopened on 2nd May 1996 and is seen on 28th April 2001, together with the long loop. *Foxcote Manor* waits with the 15.05 departure. Long term plans were to extend to Corwen. (P.G.Barnes)

BONWM HALT

43.   One mile west of Carrog was Carrog Slate Siding. The halt came into use on 21st September 1935 and was photographed not long before line closure. There was one electric light, but it was within the shelter. (Stations UK)

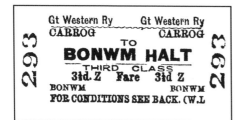

CORWEN

44.   An early postcard view of the down side features some of the staff, which numbered 33 in 1903. There were 13 in 1924. The footbridge roof was removed in the 1950s. Around 600 tons of coal arrived per annum in the early years for the Corwen Gas Light Company.
(Lens of Sutton coll.)

45.   A 1949 westward panorama includes the lofty water tank, in the right background. Nearby had been the engine shed, but this closed in 1927, and there had been a 55ft turntable.
(R.S.Carpenter coll.)

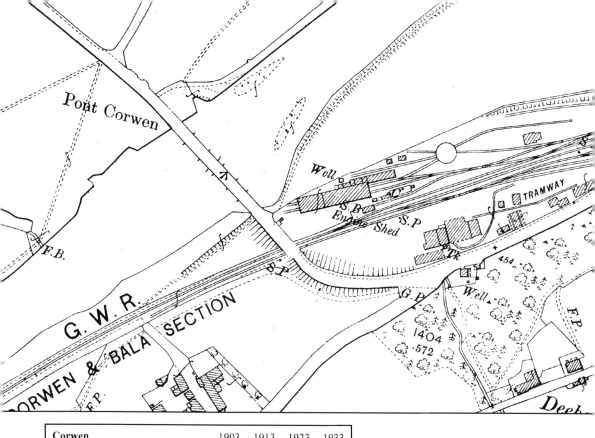

Corwen	1903	1913	1923	1933
Passenger tickets issued	42244	76163	43427	22274
Season tickets issued	*	*	136	359
Parcels forwarded	10204	12903	9715	22479
General goods forwarded (tons)	1648	1123	383	317
Coal and coke received (tons)	6184	11624	4830	2080
Other minerals received (tons)	1325	1621	4669	1712
General goods received (tons)	2826	5577	3154	2541
Coal and Coke handled	107	763	782	2728
Trucks of livestock handled	775	699	918	514

46. The engine shed had an allocation in 1901 of six 0-4-2Ts and seven 0-6-0STs. They were all GWR owned, although the shed was joint GWR/LNWR property. Three sets of LMS men were based here at the time of closure.
(W.A.Camwell/SLS coll.)

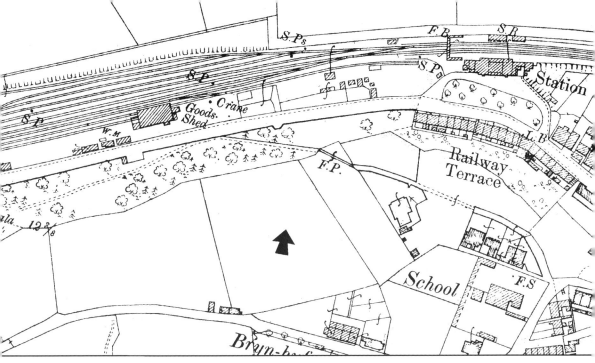

XI.   The Denbigh, Ruthin & Corwen Railway built its station beyond the right border of this 1911 map. It opened on 6th October 1864 and trains from Llangollen used a temporary one nearby until the one shown came into use in August 1865, when all trains stopped there. A future station would be near the original site. The town was immediately to the south; it housed 2723 folk in 1901, this dropping to 2048 by 1961.

47.   The 3.30pm Bala to Ruabon was propelled by 0-4-2T no. 1416 on 13th August 1953. Such autotrains often continued to Wrexham. (H.C.Casserley)

48.		Seen on the same day is 2-6-0 no. 5326 with the North Wales Land Cruise train. This popular Summer tour ran for more than ten years and included Bangor, Rhyl, Denbigh and Barmouth. Pictures and details appear in our albums on those routes, the last train running on 8th September 1961. (H.C.Casserley)

49.		The route from Denbigh had lost its passenger service in 1953 and so it was a rare treat to travel in a special from Rhyl in a new DMU. It is about to return to Llandudno in around 1956. (R.Hughes/A.M.Davies)

50.　　East Box was on the up platform and it had 35 levers. West Box was at the west end of the long loop (see map) and it had a 25-lever frame. Both were in use from 1897 to 1964. (Lens of Sutton coll.)

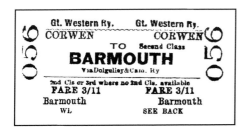

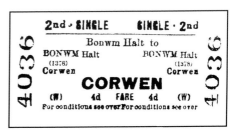

51.   A 1963 record of the prospective passengers' perspective features fine stone work. It survived demolition to become offices for Ifor Williams Trailers, the firm occupying much of the site. The station had a bookstall and refreshment room in the 1930s. (R.M.Casserley)

52.   West Box was recorded in June 1968. The turntable was behind it and this remained in use into the 1960s. The agricultural stores had a short life. There had been a saw mill on the right; it had had its own small railway and crane. Goods traffic ceased on 14th December 1964, due to the flood damage. (C.L.Caddy)

CYNWYD

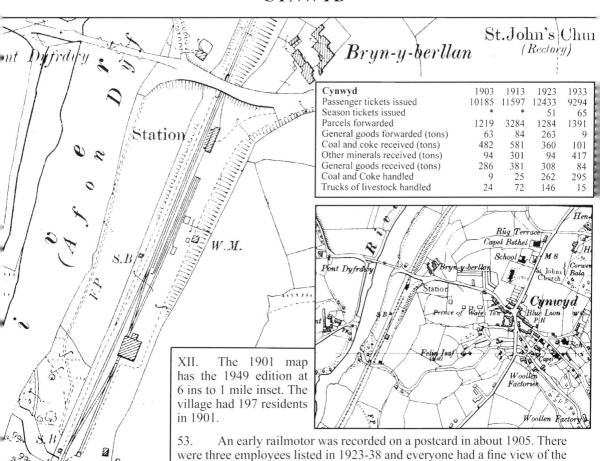

Cynwyd	1903	1913	1923	1933
Passenger tickets issued	10185	11597	12433	9294
Season tickets issued	*	*	51	65
Parcels forwarded	1219	3284	1284	1391
General goods forwarded (tons)	63	84	263	9
Coal and coke received (tons)	482	581	360	101
Other minerals received (tons)	94	301	94	417
General goods received (tons)	286	381	308	84
Coal and Coke handled	9	25	262	295
Trucks of livestock handled	24	72	146	15

XII. The 1901 map has the 1949 edition at 6 ins to 1 mile inset. The village had 197 residents in 1901.

53. An early railmotor was recorded on a postcard in about 1905. There were three employees listed in 1923-38 and everyone had a fine view of the river. (Lens of Sutton coll.)

54. The approach road and its gate are visible on the right in this northward view from July 1963. There had been a signal box present in part of the 1890s.
(R.M.Casserley)

55. A triangular roof light and three louvered openings were provided for the benefit of gentlemen and in the background can be seen the weigh house, the cattle pens and the goods shed.
(Stations UK)

56. The demolition contractor's diesel was present on 28th June 1968. The goods yard had closed on 4th May 1964 and it was provided with a one-ton crane in the shed. (C.L.Caddy)

LLANDRILLO

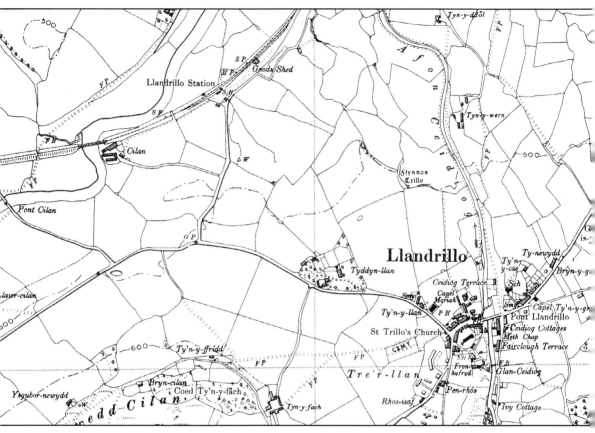

XIII.   The 1949 edition at 6ins to 1 mile is included to show the remoteness of the station from the village. This had a population of 648 in 1901 and 532 in 1961. It is on a tributary of the River Dee, which itself winds across the top left part of the map.

57.   The classic posed postcard view includes the 1897 signal box and the two-storey office on the end of the goods shed. There were two signalmen (on shifts) and a porter on the payroll in the 1903-38 period. (Lens of Sutton coll.)

58.   The main building (right) was devoid of a canopy and the spacious house for the station master was out of this 1962 view, on the right. The two sidings could accommodate 38 wagons - 29 and 9. (P.J.Garland/R.S.Carpenter coll.)

XIV.   The 1901 map shows a layout which seems not to have changed subsequently. The crane had a one-ton capacity. The signal box shown at the top just housed a ground frame.

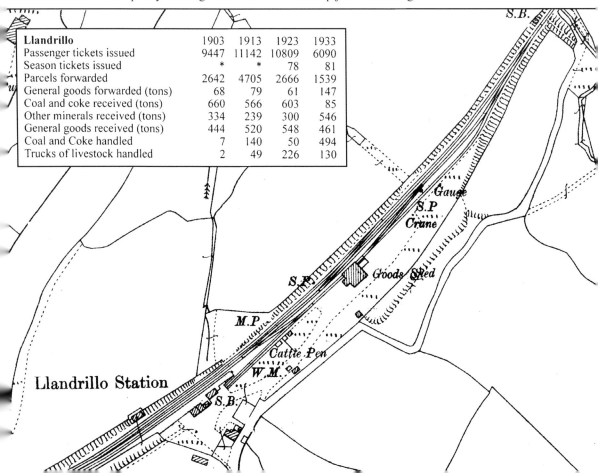

Llandrillo	1903	1913	1923	1933
Passenger tickets issued	9447	11142	10809	6090
Season tickets issued	*	*	78	81
Parcels forwarded	2642	4705	2666	1539
General goods forwarded (tons)	68	79	61	147
Coal and coke received (tons)	660	566	603	85
Other minerals received (tons)	334	239	300	546
General goods received (tons)	444	520	548	461
Coal and Coke handled	7	140	50	494
Trucks of livestock handled	2	49	226	130

59.   The 09.27 Ruabon to Barmouth was hauled by class 4 4-6-0 no. 75020 on 7th November 1964. The signal box had a 25-lever frame and lasted to the end of traffic. (E.Wilmshurst)

Transport History?

The landing of a space craft near the village at 8.38pm on 23rd January 1974 was reported widely. Furniture and ornaments moved, when a loud rumble occurred. Bright lights were seen on Cader Berwyn and the emergency services scoured the area to no avail. Reporters suggested that a UFO had called briefly, unaware that the Bala Fault had moved, with Richter 3.5 force. They also did not know that there were four meteors recorded that evening to light the sky, and these added to the confusion later that night.

Your author (VM) takes this opportunity to present a fresh explanation, having founded Bio-Gas Plant Ltd at that time. Methane is produced in anaerobic decomposition and is sometimes known as "marsh gas". Vast quantities would be released from boggy upland during an earthquake and its ignition would produce more novel lighting. Piezoelectric crystals generate sparks on compression (they are used in domestic gas igniters) and could do so in fault movement. Such sparks could set fire to the methane and no ground evidence would follow. Corwen had experienced a similar tremor in 1888, but without any fireworks. The space craft is now a local legend, which endures.

CROGEN HALL HALT

60.   The photographer was John Smith and his board is most helpful; the other one was a deterrent. The halt was private and opened in the 1920s. It was in use for only about ten years. (Lens of Sutton coll.)

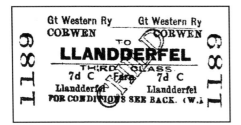

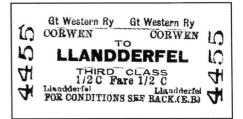

LLANDDERFEL

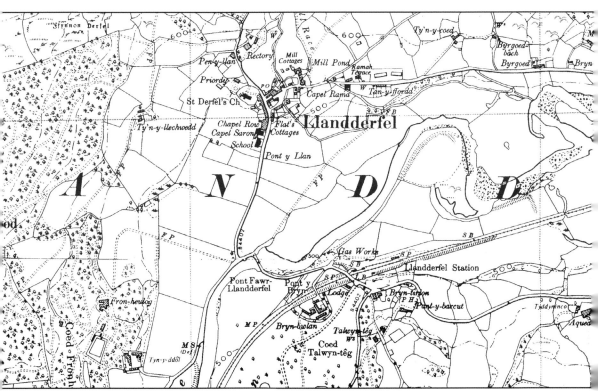

XVa   The proximity of the village to its station can be gauged on this 1949 survey at 6ins to 1 mile and once again the Dee meanders across it. The population fell from 912 in 1901 to 659 by 1961.

61.   It seems that one Edwardian postcard user felt that it needed censorship. Those posing outnumbered staff greatly; their number was the same as at the two stations eastwards. (Lens of Sutton coll.)

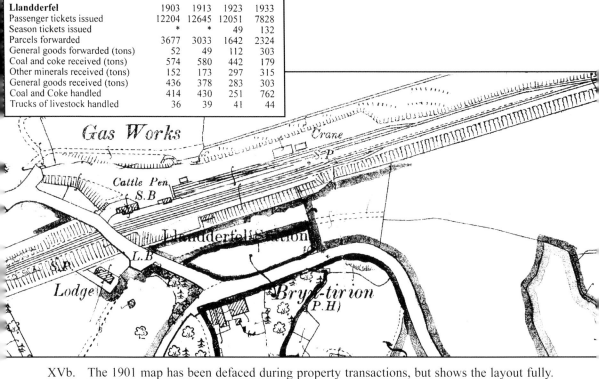

Llandderfel	1903	1913	1923	1933
Passenger tickets issued	12204	12645	12051	7828
Season tickets issued	*	*	49	132
Parcels forwarded	3677	3033	1642	2324
General goods forwarded (tons)	52	49	112	303
Coal and coke received (tons)	574	580	442	179
Other minerals received (tons)	152	173	297	315
General goods received (tons)	436	378	283	303
Coal and Coke handled	414	430	251	762
Trucks of livestock handled	36	39	41	44

XVb.   The 1901 map has been defaced during property transactions, but shows the layout fully. Beyond the right border, a signal box was shown, but it was only a ground frame. It is in the background of the next photograph. The tiny gasworks served only the larger houses.

62.   Platform lengthening is evident in this eastward panorama from March 1959. The signal box contained 14 levers and closed following track flood damage, which took place nearby. (R.M.Casserley)

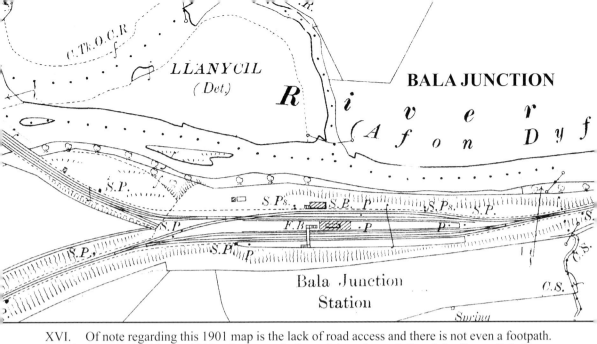

LLANYCIL
(*Det.*)

BALA JUNCTION

River Afon Dyf

Bala Junction
Station

XVI. Of note regarding this 1901 map is the lack of road access and there is not even a footpath. A path was provided in the 1920s. Our route is from right to lower left and the line to Bala Town crosses the River Dee top left. Amazingly, the stop was not shown in public timetables. The second line to Bala was termed a relief siding.

63. An eastward panorama from about 1930 includes four white posts for single line tablets. The Bala branch is on the left and thus the northern platform is the only one with a choice of destination. (Stations UK)

64.   A "Mogul" 2-6-0 heads a Birkenhead to Pwllheli train in about 1949, while a Bala service leaves in the background, hauled by a 2251 class 0-6-0. (Milepost 92½)

65.   The line in front of the signal box was used mainly for run round purposes. The locomotive is 0-6-0PT no. 7443 and it heads a train from Blaenau Ffestiniog on 18th August 1953. Passengers could not travel beyond Bala Town after 4th January 1960. (H.C.Casserley)

66.   Seen on the same day, the spacious signal box housed a massive 53-lever frame. It has signalled a departure for Bala Town and 0-4-2T no. 5810 will soon respond. (H.C.Casserley)

67.   The Pagoda shelter on the down platform is near 0-4-2T no. 5811, which is about to stop at all stations to Barmouth. An 0-6-0PT stands at the branch platform. (Lens of Sutton coll.)

68.   The 4.0pm Wrexham General to Bala Town train runs into the branch platform, probably in 1964. The 9.28pm departure did likewise. The three signals in the background show the choice of route on offer; note that up trains could not start from the down platform. Down trains to Barmouth regularly used the branch platform. (Dr. G.B.Sutton)

69.   At 8.30am in the final years, the rear coach of the 6.55 Wrexham General to Barmouth was detached and taken along the branch, mainly for the benefit of pupils of Bala Secondary School. This is taking place on the left, while 2-6-0 no. 6327 waits with the 7.18 Barmouth to Wrexham General (Dr. G.B.Sutton)

BALA LAKE HALT

70.   The station for Bala was on this site in 1868-82. The halt opened on 8th July 1935 and closed on 24th September 1939. Heading the 1.20pm Chester to Barmouth on 14th August 1962 is 4-6-0 no. 7821 *Ditcheat Manor*, which now resides on the West Somerset Railway. We have found no evidence of the halt in post-war timetables; it seems that the nameboard was replaced for the benefit of occasional Sunday excursion passengers wanting to reach Bala. (R.A.Lumber/D.H.Mitchell coll.)

4605	2nd-SINGLE	SINGLE-2nd	4605
	Llandrillo to		
	Llandrillo Bala	Llandrillo Bala	
	BALA		
	(M) 1/9 Fare 1/9 (M)		
	For conditions see over	For conditions see over	

	(65712)	(65712)	
625	2nd-SINGLE	SINGLE-2nd	625
	Bala Junction to		
	Bala Junction Bala	Bala Junction Bala	
	BALA		
	(M) 0/3 Fare 0/3 (M)		
	For conditions see over	For conditions see over	

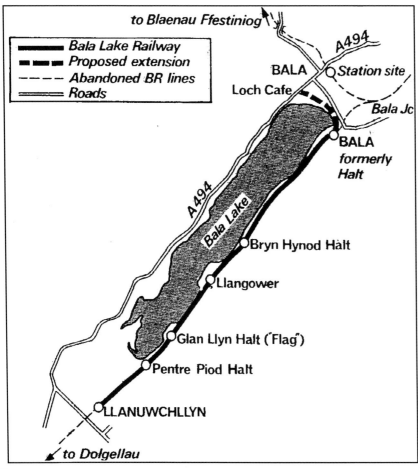

71. The durable sign and shelter were still standing on 21st June 1967. They were on the north side of the line. (C.L.Caddy)

XVII. Bala Lake Railway in 1979. The proposal, shown on the map, has not been fulfilled. (Railway Magazine)

Map legend:

▬▬▬	Bala Lake Railway
▬ ▬ ▬	Proposed extension
– – –	Abandoned BR lines
═══	Roads

to Blaenau Ffestiniog

A494

BALA

Loch Cafe

Station site

Bala Jc

BALA formerly Halt

A494

Bala Lake

Bryn Hynod Halt

Llangower

Glan Llyn Halt ('Flag')

Pentre Piod Halt

LLANUWCHLLYN

to Dolgellau

72.   The eastern terminus of the Bala Lake Railway was established in the background of the previous photograph. It is seen on 29th May 1979 with 0-4-0ST *Holy War* ready to depart with newly built coaches. As on the Talyllyn Railway, doors were required on only one side. (T.Heavyside)

73.   The footbridge from picture 71 is in the background as *Holy War* gives passengers a taste of smoke on 29th June 2008, before leaving with them. The engine was built by Hunslet in 1902. (V.Mitchell)

LLANGOWER HALT

74. The halt opened on 10th June 1929 and was photographed on 12th July 1964. There was a view of the lake from it. (C.L.Caddy)

75. The BLR built a new platform in 1972, ¼ mile west of the original, and laid a passing loop in 1978. Departing on 16th September 1978 is the 1903 Hunslet, *Maid Marian*. *Holy War* was also ex-Dinorwic Quarry. A second platform was provided in 1979. (T.Heavyside)

GLAN LLYN HALT

76.   Initially this was a private platform for Sir Watkin Wynn and called Flag station, because a flag could be raised at the adjacent cottage to summon a boat from his house across the lake. The name was shown in Bradshaw from 1926 and was regularised on 14th September 1931. It was Flag Station Halt from 4th July 1938 and became Glan Llyn Halt on 25th September 1950. (Stations UK)

77.   The unusual shelter had its back to the lake and a passing loop was provided in the early years. Some signals were retained for the use of Sir Watkin. The photograph is from July 1963. BLR trains stop here occasionally and also at their new halt, 200yds to the west, called Pentre Piod. It was opened to serve a camp site primarily. (R.M.Casserley)

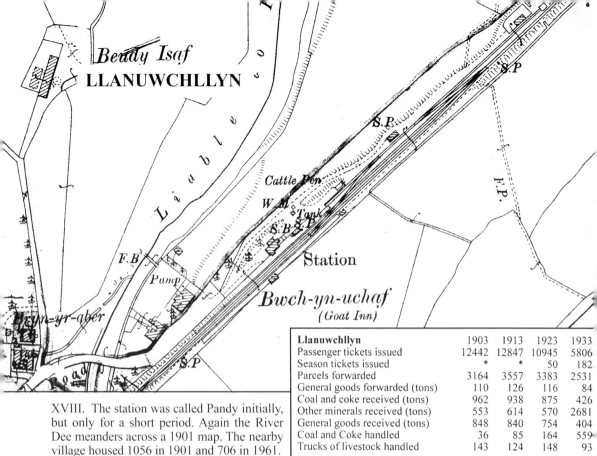

Beudy Isaf
LLANUWCHLLYN

S.P.

S.P.

Cattle Pen

W.M. *Tank*

S.B. *S.B.*

Station

F.B.

Pump

Bwch-yn-uchaf
(Goat Inn)

Bryn-yr-aber

Road

S.P.

F.P.

Llanuwchllyn	1903	1913	1923	1933
Passenger tickets issued	12442	12847	10945	5806
Season tickets issued	*	*	50	182
Parcels forwarded	3164	3557	3383	2531
General goods forwarded (tons)	110	126	116	84
Coal and coke received (tons)	962	938	875	426
Other minerals received (tons)	553	614	570	2681
General goods received (tons)	848	840	754	404
Coal and Coke handled	36	85	164	559
Trucks of livestock handled	143	124	148	93

XVIII. The station was called Pandy initially, but only for a short period. Again the River Dee meanders across a 1901 map. The nearby village housed 1056 in 1901 and 706 in 1961.

78.   This northward view is from about 1939 and features the 21-lever signal box, which survived with its frame. The goods yard remained in use until 4th August 1968. There was a staff of eight for most of the 1930s. This is the last station before the summit and banking engines often waited here. (Stations UK)

79.   A photograph from July 1963 features a Barmouth to Chester train leaving behind class 4 4-6-0 no. 75006. Note that there is a "parachute" water tank on each platform. On the left is a "cow horn" to receive the single line tablet and beyond it is the lamp hut.
(J.W.T.House/C.L.Caddy coll.)

80.   The platform canopy initially served at Pwllheli's first station and was then moved to Aberdovey from where it was recovered to serve here. This view is from the former down platform in October 2004 and includes the BLR workshops in the distance. (P.O'Callaghan)

81.　　A panorama from the up platform on 29th June 2008 shows more of the original southwest elevation, plus diesel *Bob Davies* with stock for the first morning departure. The necessary car park is largely out of view on the left. The wooden cafe building had come from Barmouth Junction. (V.Mitchell)

82.　　Seen on the same day is the main workshop with 0-4-0ST *Holy War* moving towards the station to haul the first train of the day. The building also serves as a running shed. The permanent way stock is on the left. (V.Mitchell)

LLYS HALT

83. Opening on 4th June 1934, the halt was built on the south side of the line. There was a house to the left of the camera in which the crossing keeper resided. The photograph is from July 1964. (C.L.Caddy)

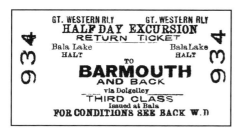

GARNEDDWEN HALT

84.   A passing loop was laid in 1913 at the summit of the route, which is at 760ft above sea level. In the final years, only one pair of trains passed here and then on Summer Saturdays only. The up one called at 1.55pm. The platforms came into use on 9th July 1928 and were reached by a footpath across the fields. (Dr G.B.Sutton)

85.   Goods trains were required to stop here to have wagon brakes pinned down. Some were hauled by 2-8-0s in 1939-44. The signal box had 22 levers and was often switched out, closing permanently on 4th November 1963. We are looking west at the start of the descent. (Stations UK)

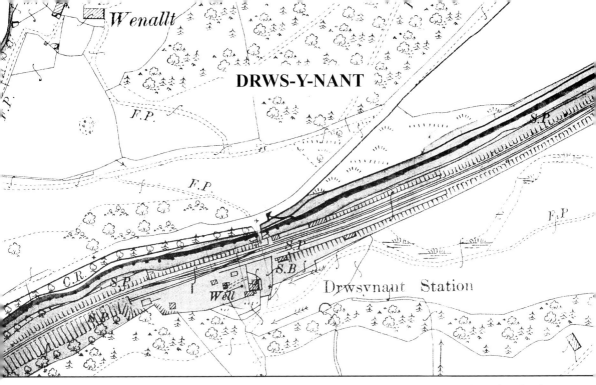

DRWS-Y-NANT

Wenallt

Drwsynant Station

XIX. The 1901 edition contains the long passing loop, the up side of which has the points for the short siding. This was in use until 4th May 1964. The main road is close by.

86. This is the 4.20pm from Dolgelley, which was booked to return there at 5.00, not Saturdays or school holidays. It ran until the line closed. The siding and signal box are on the left. The latter had 23 levers and lasted until line closure. The level crossing was close to it. (Dr G.B.Sutton)

Drws-y-Nant	1903	1913	1923	1933
Passenger tickets issued	3922	4201	4712	1574
Season tickets issued	*	*	36	14
Parcels forwarded	827	1562	778	424
General goods forwarded (tons)	64	27	343	13
Coal and coke received (tons)	166	153	100	86
Other minerals received (tons)	91	274	275	245
General goods received (tons)	385	308	389	38
Coal and Coke handled	67	71	96	138
Trucks of livestock handled	15	15	11	17

87.　　It is 12th July 1964 and perfect tranquility prevails. There were two men listed here in the 1929-38 period. The gradient through the station was 1 in 64, so wagons were run into the siding under gravity. (C.L.Caddy)

WNION HALT

88.　　We look north in January 1962 in a particularly narrow part of Wnion Valley. The halt was a latecomer, not opening until 5th June 1933. (A.M.Davies)

BONTNEWYDD

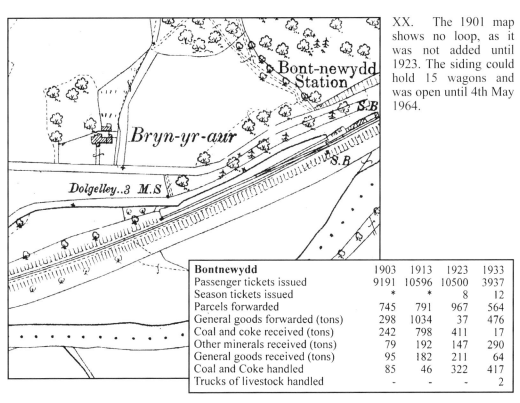

XX. The 1901 map shows no loop, as it was not added until 1923. The siding could hold 15 wagons and was open until 4th May 1964.

Bontnewydd	1903	1913	1923	1933
Passenger tickets issued	9191	10596	10500	3937
Season tickets issued	*	*	8	12
Parcels forwarded	745	791	967	564
General goods forwarded (tons)	298	1034	37	476
Coal and coke received (tons)	242	798	411	17
Other minerals received (tons)	79	192	147	290
General goods received (tons)	95	182	211	64
Coal and Coke handled	85	46	322	417
Trucks of livestock handled	-	-	-	2

89.   The siding is in the distance in this 1930s view. The new platform was built of timber, as it was on made-up ground on the valley side. The shelter was on stilts. (Stations UK)

90.   A 1962 view has a road junction in the distance; the one near us turns left, descending to the bont newydd, Welsh for new bridge. The box opened on 5th August 1923 and had a 20-lever frame. (P.J.Garland/R.S.Carpenter coll.)

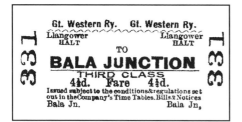

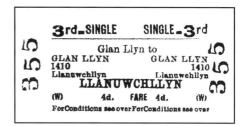

DOLSERAU HALT

91.   The halt opened late (8th February 1935) and closed early (29th October 1951). The sign carries the suffix FOR THE TORRENT WALK and was on the north side of the line. In addition to the two school trains in 1948, there was a 9.22am to Barmouth, every weekday, and a 7.52pm arrival, but this was Saturdays only. (R.M.Casserley coll.)

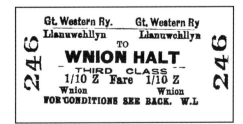

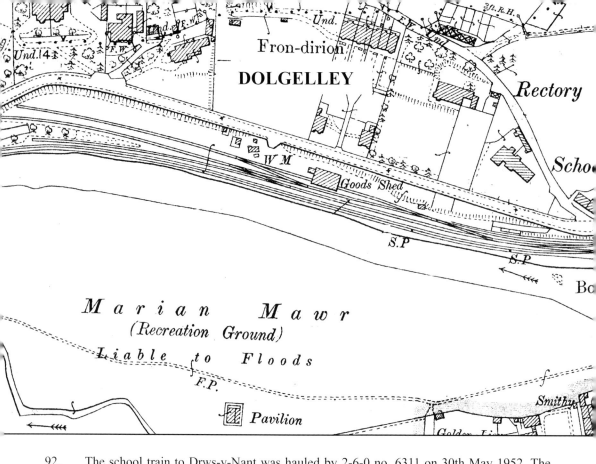

Fron-dirion

DOLGELLEY

Rectory

Sch

WM

Goods Shed

S.P

S.P

Bo

Marian   Mawr
(Recreation Ground)
Liable to Floods

F.P.

Pavilion

Smithy

Golden Li

92.   The school train to Drws-y-Nant was hauled by 2-6-0 no. 6311 on 30th May 1952. The canopy styles reflect the earlier different ownerships. This is shown on the map. (R.A.Lumber/D.H.Mitchell coll.)

XXI.   The CR and the GWR stations are identified on the 1911 edition. The CR had a temporary terminus at the west end of the goods yard from 21st June until 1st August 1869. The turntable was 42ft long and is right centre. Further right is East Box, its 25 levers being in use from 1894 to 1922. It was then used as a porters cabin. The station spelling was Dolgelly until around 1896 and Dolgellau from 12th September 1960. There was a staff of 17 to 19 in 1923-38. The number of residents was steady at around 2400 in that era. Also marked is the works of the Dolgelley Gas & Coke Company, which was established in 1855. It closed in 1959, when gas was piped from Barmouth. In its final year, 1300 tons of coal came by rail for gas production.

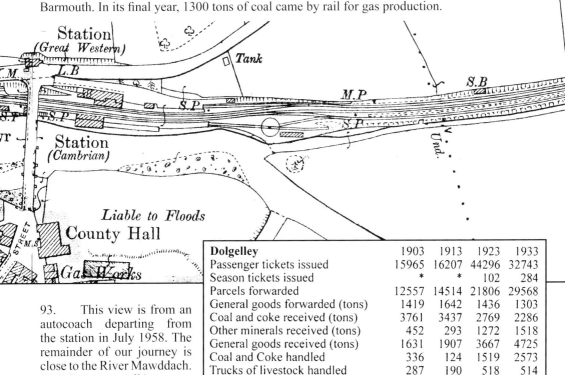

93.   This view is from an autocoach departing from the station in July 1958. The remainder of our journey is close to the River Mawddach. (R.S.Carpenter coll.)

Dolgelley	1903	1913	1923	1933
Passenger tickets issued	15965	16207	44296	32743
Season tickets issued	*	*	102	284
Parcels forwarded	12557	14514	21806	29568
General goods forwarded (tons)	1419	1642	1436	1303
Coal and coke received (tons)	3761	3437	2769	2286
Other minerals received (tons)	452	293	1272	1518
General goods received (tons)	1631	1907	3667	4725
Coal and Coke handled	336	124	1519	2573
Trucks of livestock handled	287	190	518	514

DOLGELLAU

94.   This panorama is in the other direction and includes the lines to the goods yard on the right. It had a 6-ton crane and closed on 4th May 1964. West Box (21 levers) had been in the left foreground until 1922. (R.S.Carpenter)

95.   The picture was taken from the top of the sloping footway from the down platform on 7th November 1964. No. 46521 is working the 1.41pm local train to Barmouth. The riverside siding had a six-wheeled six-berthed camp coach in 1935-39. (E.Wilmshurst)

96.   The dock near the water tank could take four wagons and on the other side of the running lines was a siding for 35 wagons or a terminating train. The 1922 replacement signal box is on the right, it having 35 levers. The old CR box on the left had 19 and had closed in 1894, but was still in good order in September 1963, devoid of rods. (R.S.Carpenter coll.)

97.   It is July 1964 and the end was nigh. The enterprising GWR had introduced steam railcars here in 1922, most running to Barmouth, but some terminated at Harlech. They were replaced by autotrains in 1927. (C.L.Caddy)

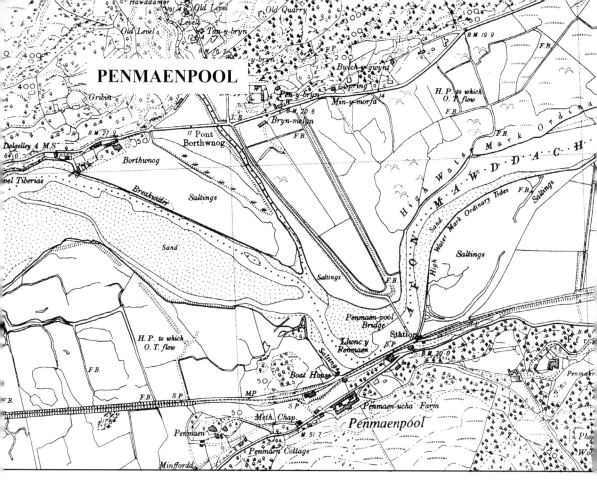

PENMAENPOOL

XXII. The 6ins to 1 mile map of 1949 shows the toll bridge immediately north of the station and the road to be on an embankment across the estuary. There were several gold mines still worked in foothills on the north shore.

98. The white railings of the toll bridge are on the right in this view from about 1962. The signalman has the tablet hoop ready for the driver of the 10.20am Barmouth to Chester, which is hauled by 4-6-0 no. 75006. (J.W.T.House/C.L.Caddy coll.)

99.   On the left of this panorama from 16th July 1963 is the toll hut and opposite it is the office. Opposite the 1936 25-lever signal box is the roofless weigh house. The box became an information office for the RSPB in 1976 and is well conserved now. It had been on show at the British Empire Exhibition at Wembley in 1924. (R.M.Casserley)

XXIII. The 1901 extract includes the CR's engine shed lower left and the restricted goods yard top right. It closed on 4th May 1964. The toll bridge was built in 1879.

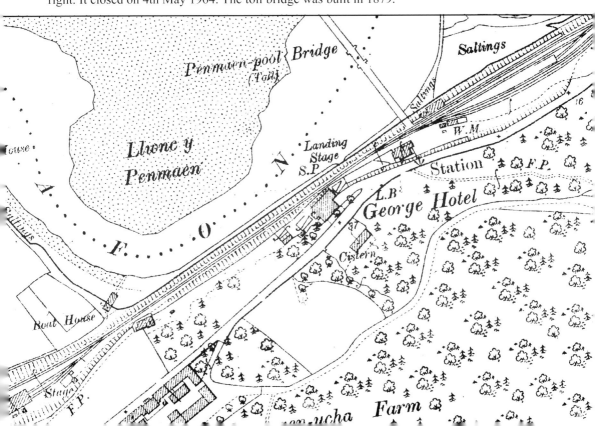

100.   Four sets of engine men were still listed here at the time of shed closure in January 1965. Seen on 12th July 1964 are 2-6-0 no. 46521 and 4-6-0 no. 75029. Both engines were subsequently preserved. The concrete columns support the water tank. The shed codes were sub to 84J until January 1961, 89B to September 1963 and finally 6C. (C.L.Caddy)

Penmaenpool	1923	1933
Passenger tickets issued	16031	8232
Season tickets issued	36	82
Parcels forwarded	1357	1071
General goods forwarded (tons)	386	-
Coal and coke received (tons)	136	86
Other minerals received (tons)	706	141
General goods received (tons)	655	79
Coal and Coke handled	428	274
Trucks of livestock handled	5	-

101.   Seen on 27th November 1964 is 4-6-0 no. 75020 with the 8.45am Chester to Barmouth train. It is leaving the down platform, which was a late addition. Near the period car is the small goods shed and beyond that are three coal wagons. (D.A.Johnson)

102.   On the left are the former station offices and the bedroom of the house is evident beyond. The building was remote from, and lower than, the platforms, despite the sign to the contrary. The trackbed now carries a roadway ornamented by signals, although the originals were bidirectional. (B.W.L.Brooksbank)

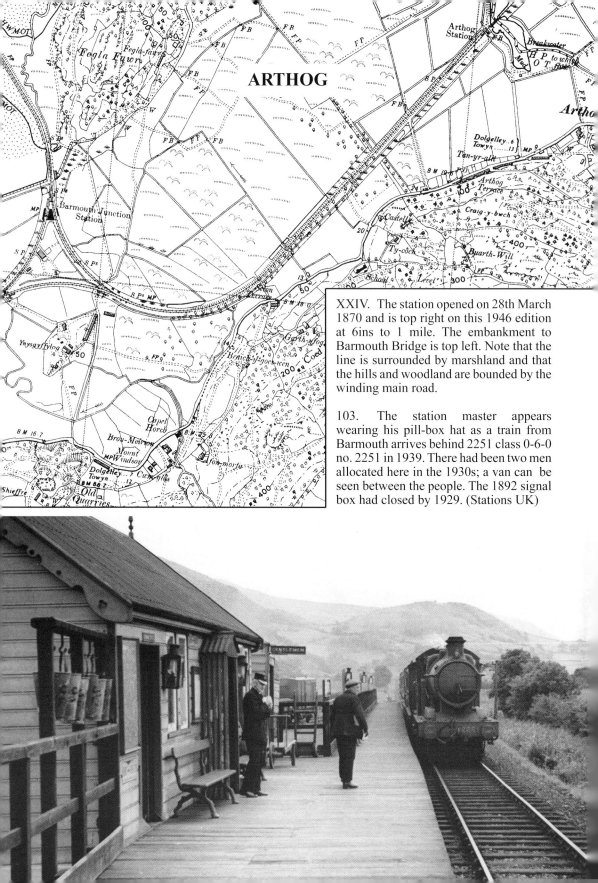

ARTHOG

XXIV. The station opened on 28th March 1870 and is top right on this 1946 edition at 6ins to 1 mile. The embankment to Barmouth Bridge is top left. Note that the line is surrounded by marshland and that the hills and woodland are bounded by the winding main road.

103. The station master appears wearing his pill-box hat as a train from Barmouth arrives behind 2251 class 0-6-0 no. 2251 in 1939. There had been two men allocated here in the 1930s; a van can be seen between the people. The 1892 signal box had closed by 1929. (Stations UK)

104. The Cardiff property developer, Solomon Andrews, had a success at Pwllheli and began a leisure resort on the waterfront half mile west of Arthog station. However, only this part of the frontage was built and it survives today as Jubilee Terrace. The tramway was short lived and was of 3ft gauge. It brought stone from the quarry lower left on map XXIV and had one frame carrying a body from Andrews Cardiff Tramway. Two new cars were ordered, but went into use on his Pwllheli & Llanbedrog Tramway instead. Services were provided from here to Barmouth Junction and to the end of the footway on Barmouth Bridge in the Summer of 1903, probably the only year of passenger operation. (Andrews Archive)

Arthog	1923	1933
Passenger tickets issued	8122	8925
Season tickets issued	16	46
Parcels forwarded	1186	1052
General goods forwarded (tons)	5	3
Coal and coke received (tons)	46	30
Other minerals received (tons)	60	153
General goods received (tons)	135	133
Coal and Coke handled	119	156
Trucks of livestock handled	-	-

105. The trackbed along the estuary now forms the Mawddach Trail, but there is no trace of the station. This view west is from 16th July 1962 and includes a camping coach. The goods yard closed on 4th May 1964. (J.Langford)

106. The proximity of the river is evident in the background of this panorama from late 1962. Erosion of the embankment was an ongoing expensive problem for about four miles, but the views were excellent. The gents (right) was prone to sink into the marshland. (P.J.Garland/R.S.Carpenter)

XXV. The 1947 edition at 1ins to 1 mile has Penmaenpool top right, plus the final 6½ miles of our journey. Close examination lower left will reveal the Fairbourne Miniature Railway, which still prospered in 2010.

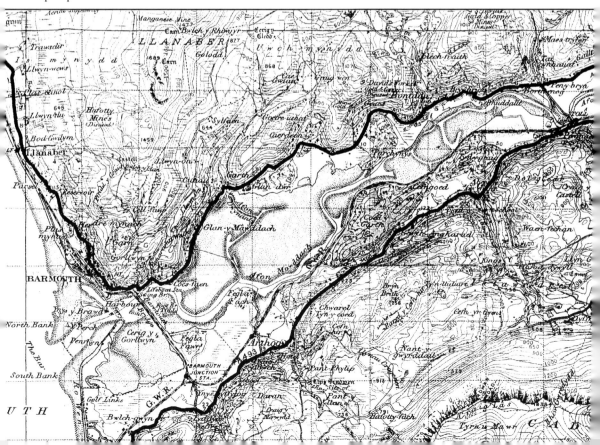

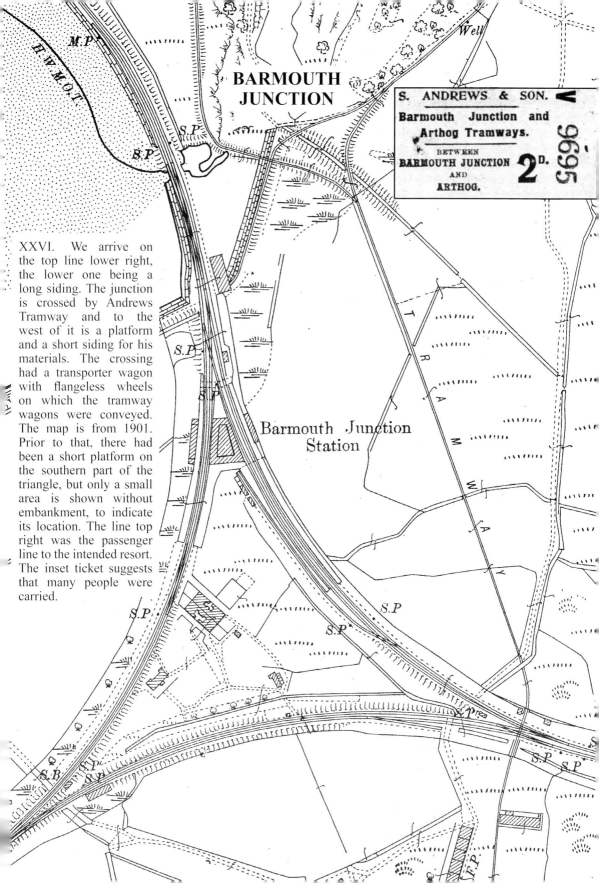

**BARMOUTH
JUNCTION**

XXVI. We arrive on the top line lower right, the lower one being a long siding. The junction is crossed by Andrews Tramway and to the west of it is a platform and a short siding for his materials. The crossing had a transporter wagon with flangeless wheels on which the tramway wagons were conveyed. The map is from 1901. Prior to that, there had been a short platform on the southern part of the triangle, but only a small area is shown without embankment, to indicate its location. The line top right was the passenger line to the intended resort. The inset ticket suggests that many people were carried.

Barmouth Junction Station

107. Andrews built a large refreshment room with toilets close to the northern apex of the triangle and it was here that his public tram service started. Work began here in 1899, but the entire project ended in 1906. The shed is on the map.
(Andrews Archive)

108. This is East Box, which was in use from 1892 to 1931 and it was photographed in 1917. The up building can be seen under the handrail. (C.C.Green coll.)

109.   Barmouth Bridge is in the background and a train is approaching it. Curving on the right is the eastern side of the triangular junction. The southern part was used for the exchange of freight traffic and the entire triangle was used for the turning of locomotives too big for the Barmouth turntable. (J.Langford coll.)

MORFA MAWDDACH

110.   This was the name from 13th June 1960 and two years later we look at the Cambrian Coast line platforms, which were numbered 3 and 4. Only No. 3 remains in use, it having been rebuilt and raised in 1986. All the buildings were demolished in 1971.
(P.J.Garland/R.S.Carpenter coll.)

111.   Seen from platform 1 sometime in 1962 is 4-6-0 no. 75023 with the 7.17am Ruabon to Barmouth. A camping coach is in the bay platform, which was once used by local trains to Dolgelley. The GWR first allocated a camp coach (not camp*ing*) here in 1934.
(J.W.T.House/C.L.Caddy coll.)

112.   It is May 1963 and another class 4 creeps off the bridge, which was (and is) subject to severe speed restrictions. The signal box had 38 levers and functioned until 15th June 1968. Goods traffic ceased here on 4th November 1963. (C.L.Caddy.)

SOUTH OF BARMOUTH

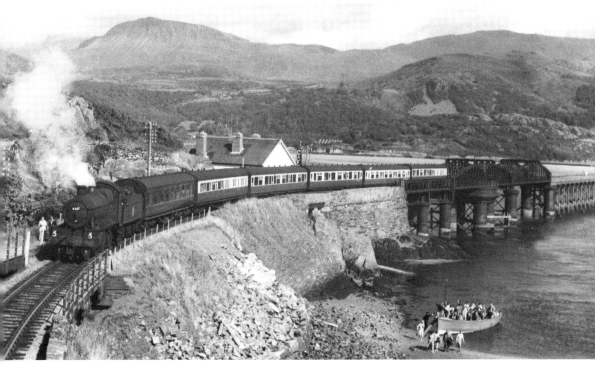

113.	The dark part of the bridge includes a swing span, which replaced a drawbridge in 1899.
No. 6367, a 4300 class 2-6-0, is heading the 3.15pm Wrexham to Barmouth in July 1957. The rear
of the third coach is on the bridge over the lifeboat slipway, which passed through the embankment
and was in use from 1859 until 2004. (J.W.T.House/C.L.Caddy coll.)

114.	A photograph from 20th August 1966 has the locomotive in the same position, but we look
in the other direction at Porkington Terrace Tunnel, which is 70yds long. (A.M.Davies)

115. On emerging from the tunnel, the line crosses Old Chapel Viaduct (78 yds). It was rebuilt in concrete in 1952, but parts of the original timber structure (lower left) were still visible in 2008. The timber of the main bridge was found to be defective in October 1980 and closure for seven months for temporary repairs followed. Completion took until April 1986 and a major strengthening followed, this being finalised in 2003. (V.Mitchell)

116. A further curve followed and trains reached double track leading to the station. No. 75021 is heading the 11.10 Paddington to Pwllheli on 7th August 1965. The length of the bridge it has just crossed is 600yds. It carries a footpath, which is subject to a toll.
(R.A.Lumber/D.H.Mitchell coll.)

BARMOUTH

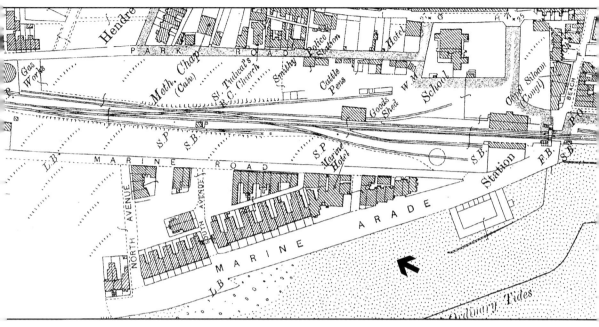

XXVII. The map is from 1913 and thus it does not show the extra platform added south of the level crossing in about 1924. The scale is 20ins to 1 mile.

117.   The additional platform was termed "Excursion Platform", but was in practice a bay platform, mainly for Dolgelley trains. Its substantial shelter is evident, as no. 3224 departs south. The 3206 class of 2-4-0s were known as "Barnums" and date from 1889. (R.M.Casserley coll.)

118.   No. 78003 arrives with a train from Birkenhead, while the running round of a local train is in progress. On the right is South Box, which had 27 levers and a gate wheel. It worked until 22nd October 1988 and it was moved to the Llangollen Railway ten years later. It was rebuilt at the Carrog end of Glyndyfrdwy station as an information centre. (J.W.T.House/C.L.Caddy coll.)

119.   Standing at the bay platform on 11th July 1964 is 2-6-0 no. 46521 with a short train for Dolgellau. The platform was little used after the end of steam and all the trackwork was simplified in 1974. (C.L.Caddy)

120.   A final overview from the north includes the carriage sidings and the site of the goods yard. North Box served until 29th September 1974. All these features were lost, but we can rejoice that trains still run and at an improved frequency. (C.L.Caddy)

Other views can be found in *Machynlleth to Barmouth* and *Barmouth to Pwllheli*.

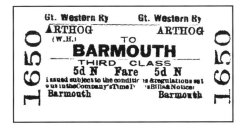

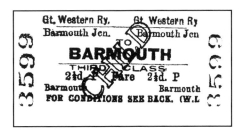

MP Middleton Press

EVOLVING THE ULTIMATE RAIL ENCYCLOPEDIA

Easebourne Lane, Midhurst, West Sussex.
GU29 9AZ   Tel:01730 813169

www.middletonpress.co.uk   email:info@middletonpress.co.uk
A-978 0 906520   B-978 1 873793   C-978 1 901706   D-978 1 904474   E-978 1 906008

All titles listed below were in print at time of publication - please check current availability by looking at our website - www.middletonpress.co.uk or by requesting a Brochure which includes our LATEST RAILWAY TITLES also our TRAMWAY, TROLLEYBUS, MILITARY and WATERWAYS series